REFERENCE

CULTURES OF THE WORLD

BRITAIN

Barbara Fuller

MARSHALL CAVENDISH
New York • London • Sydney

Reference edition published 1994 by
Marshall Cavendish Corporation
2415 Jerusalem Avenue
P.O. Box 587
North Bellmore
New York 11710

© Times Editions Pte Ltd 1994

Originated and designed by
Times Books International, an imprint of
Times Editions Pte Ltd

Printed in Singapore

Library of Congress Cataloging-in-Publication Data:
Fuller, Barbara, 1961–
    Britain / Barbara Fuller. — Reference ed.
      p. cm.—(Cultures Of The World)
    Includes bibliographical references.
    ISBN 1-85435-585-6 (set). — ISBN 1-85435-587-2 (vol.)
    1. Great Britain—Juvenile literature. [1. Great Britain.]
I. Title. II. Series.
DA27.5.F85 1994
941—dc20   93–45745
                          CIP
                           AC

Cultures of the World
Editorial Director	Shirley Hew
Managing Editor	Shova Loh
Editors	Tan Kok Eng
	Roseline Lum
	Michael Spilling
	Winnifred Wong
	Guek-Cheng Pang
	Sue Sismondo
Picture Editor	Mee-Yee Lee
Production	Edmund Lam
Design	Tuck Loong
	Ronn Yeo
	Felicia Wong
	Loo Chuan Ming
Illustrators	Eric Chew
	Lok Kerk Hwang
	William Sim
	Wong Nok Sze
MCC Editorial Director	Evelyn M. Fazio

INTRODUCTION

 Britain, a shortened term for Great Britain, is the largest of the 2,000 or so islands that make up the British Isles. Britain is part of the United Kingdom. The U.K. also includes Northern Ireland. The Isle of Man and the Channel Islands (Jersey, Guernsey, Alderney, and Sark) are Crown dependencies with their own legislative systems for domestic affairs, and are technically not part of the United Kingdom. Within Britain are the countries of England, Wales, and Scotland.

The flag of Great Britain, the Union Flag, is the same as that of the United Kingdom: England's red cross of St. George, combined with Scotland's diagonal white cross on a blue background of St. Andrew, and with Ireland's red diagonal cross of St. Patrick. Each part of the kingdom has its own heraldic device: Scotland has a thistle, England a rose, and Wales a leek.

CONTENTS

The handsome uniform of the Queen's personal guards.

CONTENTS

Costumes worn at the annual Lord Mayor's Show.

GEOGRAPHY

GREAT BRITAIN IS LOCATED between 50° and 60° north latitude, and at zero degree longitude. It is 600 miles at its longest point from the north of Scotland to the south coast of England, 300 miles at the widest point from the west of Wales to the east coast, and from John O'Groats at the northeastern tip of Scotland, to Land's End at the westernmost tip of Cornwall, is 874 miles. England is 50,056 square miles in area; Scotland is 29,794 square miles; and Wales is 7,967 square miles. Britain's total population is approximately 55.5 million, mostly concentrated in the southeast, particularly in the Greater London area.

The British Isles were separated from the continent of Europe at the end of the last Ice Age, when temperatures rose and the ice cap melted, flooding the shallow shelf of what is now the North Sea and the English Channel.

PHYSICAL GEOGRAPHY

The main geological structures of Europe continue westward to Britain: the great plain of northern Europe reappears as the windswept lowlands of eastern England, and north of these lowlands are remnants of Scandinavian mountains split by rift valleys. The fjords of Norway are repeated in the indented west Scottish coasts; ria coasts (coastal inlets) like those of Spain and Brittany are found in South Wales; the German and Dutch estuaries and shores are echoed in eastern England, with submerged river mouths and wide shallow bays; and the white cliffs of Dover in Kent mirror those of Picardy in France, only 20 miles away across the English Channel. Britain's highlands lie in the north and west, with a central belt of lowland farther east.

Opposite: **Land's End in Cornwall is the extreme southwesterly tip of England. The Cornish coast is noted for its rugged beauty.**

Above: **The white cliffs of Dover in the county of Kent on the southeastern coast.**

7

EAST ANGLIA Norfolk, Suffolk, Cambridgeshire, and Essex make up Britain's eastern bulge, known as East Anglia. Rarely rising above 300 feet, the drained fens and broken-down glacial deposits make fertile arable land. Cereals and cash crops such as sugar beets, potatoes, and other vegetables are grown in rotation here, as this region has the lowest annual rainfall in Britain. The Norfolk Broads are popular for sailing and cruising. The east coast suffers from erosion, as well as some sedimentation. Norwich and Cambridge are historic cities in the region.

The Norfolk Broads are the result of 12th-century peat cutting: people used this decayed marsh vegetation for fuel when other resources were scarce. Over 2,500 acres were dug during this period. The area is traversed by inland waterways, and it is a popular holiday center for boating enthusiasts from all over Britain.

THE SOUTH COAST The chalk ridges of Kent's North Downs and Sussex's South Downs run parallel in an east-west direction and are broken by north- or south-flowing streams. They face inward over the weald, a concentric series of clay valleys and sandstone ridges, where major crops are fruit and hops used in the brewing industry. The Hampshire Basin is ringed by chalk hills. Coastal resort towns include Bognor Regis and Brighton, with its famous pier and Royal Pavilion. Canterbury in Kent has England's main Anglican cathedral.

THE HOME COUNTIES London's suburban sprawl stretches out towards more picturesque villages in the surrounding counties. The Chiltern hills rise to 800 feet and have colorful beech woods; the valley of the Thames River extends from the river's source in Gloucestershire through Henley-on-Thames to the royal castle at Windsor and beyond to London.

THE WEST COUNTRY The monoliths of Stonehenge are a popular tourist attraction on the chalk downs of the Salisbury Plain. Dorset's moody countryside of verdant pasture land and barren heaths is described in the

novels of Thomas Hardy, while the limestones and fossils of Lulworth Cove on its coast are a geologist's dream. Devon's pretty coastal towns contrast with the classic granite moorlands of Exmoor and Dartmoor, which have rocky tors(pinnacles) and upland plateaus. The Cornish coast is more rugged than Devon's, and is a popular tourist area.

On the northern edge of the Somerset Plain are the Mendip hills where Cheddar Gorge—famous for caving, rock climbing, and cheese—is located. The Vale of Evesham's mild climate is ideal for growing fruit and vegetables. Golden-colored oolite stone makes for picturesque towns and villages in the Cotswolds: Burford and Oxford are examples. Bath is an 18th-century spa town with well-proportioned streets where the Georgian gentry sought health cures; its thermal baths date from Roman times.

WALES The principality of Wales is 135 miles long and 35 miles wide. The Black Mountains and the Brecon Beacons are rugged mountainous regions of South Wales, the latter rising to 2,000 feet. The coast of Pembrokeshire is a national park, home to numerous seabirds. Merthyr

Tors(rocky pinnacles) deposited by glaciers from the last Ice Age are a common feature in Dartmoor, Devon.

Tydfil lies within a large coalfield: mining is now on the decline, as are the supporting heavy iron and steel industries in the region. Cardiff and Swansea are major cities of South Wales.

Most of the uplands of central Wales are drained by the River Wye. To the east, the Welsh plateau breaks up into the Welsh border hills, cut through by the Severn Valley.

North Wales is more agricultural than the south. Sheep farming is the most effective use of this area characterized by high and glaciated uplands. Mount Snowdon is 3,561 feet high, accessible by mountain railway as well as by walking trails. Welsh knitwear and woven fabrics from the upland regions are renowned for their quality. Ferries leave Holyhead on the Isle of Anglesey for Dublin in Ireland.

THE MIDLANDS Much of Britain's industrial development took place in the low plateaus of the Midlands, particularly in the areas near the Nottingham and Leicester coalfield known as the Black Country. Coventry was a center of the automobile industry; near Telford, the Ironbridge

Museum of the Industrial Revolution has an interesting collection of industrial inventions. Warwick Castle, dating from the 14th century, is one of England's most important medieval castles; Stratford-upon-Avon, Shakespeare's birthplace, boasts Tudor-style black-and-white buildings, as well as the renowned Royal Shakespeare Company's Swan Theatre. Along the east coast, the flat arable land of Lincolnshire stretches north from the Wash up to the Humber estuary.

THE PEAK DISTRICT Britain's first national park, a horseshoe ring of sandstone ridge surrounding a limestone plateau with southeast flowing rivers, is bordered by Nottingham, Stoke-on-Trent, Greater Manchester, and Sheffield. Its wild moorlands and craggy rocks are popular with climbers and walkers. The 250-mile long Pennine Way footpath starts here.

Northwest of the Peak District lies Lancashire; to its east over the Pennine Hills is Yorkshire. An age-old rivalry between the counties, based on two families' claims to the English throne, dates from the 15th century. Two national parks lie in Yorkshire: the North York Moors National Park and the Yorkshire Dales National Park.

Warwick Castle in Warwickshire, near Coventry. Most of the present building dates back to the 14th and 15th century.

Loch Ness. The earliest known reference to the Loch Ness monster was in St. Adamman's biography of St. Columba in the 7th century. Interest revived in the 1930s, and sporadic attempts to photograph or find the monster continue.

THE NORTHEAST County Durham lies on a coalfield, with steel and other heavy industries in Consett. It is also traversed by the rugged moorlands of the Pennines. Durham is a medival university town, centered around a cathedral on a steep hill encircled by a river. Newcastle-upon-Tyne was an important shipbuilding port, now in economic decline. To the north of Newcastle lies Northumbria, where Hadrian's Wall, completed in A.D. 136, stretches for 73 miles across England from Wallsend, Tyne-and-Wear to Bowness-on-Solway. Sheep farming and forestry are the main forms of agriculture in the region.

SCOTLAND Scotland's Southern Uplands encompass the border area and the southern region with undulating pastoral farming land. Farther north, the large cities of Edinburgh on the Firth of Forth on the east coast, and Glasgow on the west, are sited 45 miles apart at Scotland's narrowest neck. These cities are in the Central Lowlands that reach up to the Sidlaw and Ochil Hills of Strathmore.

THE LAKE DISTRICT

A mountainous region of radial hills interspersed with glaciated lake-filled troughs to the north of Lancashire in northwest England proves a year-round attraction to tourists. Lake Windermere is popular for pleasure cruises and boating activities; climbers attempt the 3,210 foot Scafell Pikes, or the lesser peaks of Skiddaw or Helvellyn. Walkers and hikers abound in this picturesque region that has inspired many poets.

The Grampian mountains form the division between the Lowlands and the Highlands in Scotland. Aberdeen is an important oil processing town for the North Sea oil and gas fields. The islands of Jura and Islay, to the north of the Firth of Clyde, are renowned whisky-producing areas; thick woolen knitwear comes from the nearby Isle of Aran. Cut into the highland plateau, large glens—bleak and almost barren valleys—often have cool lakes, called "lochs." Loch Ness, stretching in a southwest direction through Glen More, from near Inverness on the east coast towards Fort Augustus, is reputed to harbor a prehistoric monster. Britain's highest mountain, the 4,406-foot Ben Nevis, is nearby.

To the north of Glen More lie the North West Highlands, where the population density drops to 6 persons per square mile. In the uplands many people are tenant farmers. With small farms of 5 to 10 acres, they grow oats and potatoes and keep chickens. Besides farming, knitwear and tweed manufacture are the local industries, while salmon and trout fishing, grouse shooting, and deer stalking (hunting) are lucrative tourist attractions as well as popular pastimes for residents.

Tower Bridge spans the Thames east of the City, near the Tower of London. The bridge was completed in 1894; the lower section opens to allow large ships to pass below.

CITIES

Britain's cities act as regional and cultural centers: a few of the larger ones are described in this section.

LONDON Britain's capital city is a center of international trade and finance, tourism, retailing, and government services. The original City of London is the financial center. Located within its square mile are the Bank of England, the Stock Exchange, Lloyds of London (insurance underwriters), and the headquarters of major banks. To the east of this area lies the Tower of London; farther east is the East End, formerly a center of the textile industry.

By contrast, the West End is the entertainment district: many theaters are located near Piccadilly Circus and Shaftesbury Avenue; Leicester Square has numerous cinemas; Oxford Street and nearby streets are shopping areas; Covent Garden has a prestigious opera house and a flourishing arts market.

The Houses of Parliament overlook the River Thames in Westminster. Big Ben, a large clock tower, rises on the north side of the building. Westminster Abbey, located across the street, was founded by King Edward the Confessor in 1065. Government offices and ministries are found in Whitehall, with the residences of the prime minister and the Chancellor of the Exchequer on Downing Street. The Mall leads from Trafalgar Square to Buckingham Palace. The British Museum and University College London are in the Bloomsbury area between West End and the City.

The Wellington Shambles Inn in the center of Manchester.

BIRMINGHAM Britain's second largest city is sited in the middle of England. It is a center of light and medium industry such as metals and engineering, automobiles and bicycles, and machine tools. Many traditional industries are now in decline. Birmingham also has two universities and a symphony orchestra.

MANCHESTER Manchester has a population of half a million, but 3.5 million live in the Greater Manchester area. The city was wealthy in Victorian times, deriving its wealth from the cotton trade and its associated industries. With a decline in world demand and increasing foreign competition, Manchester has experienced a downturn. Manchester is a regional banking center and the home of the Northern Stock Exchange.

EDINBURGH Edinburgh Castle dominates the Scottish capital, looking out over the Royal Mile, a street of beautiful 16th- and 17th- century townhouses that runs from the castle to the palace of Holyroodhouse, the Queen's official Scottish residence. Edinburgh has two universities and a growing computer industry. Other industries include engineering, food

City of Glasgow. After a severe economic decline during the 1970s when key manufacturing and shipbuilding industries were virtually destroyed, Glasgow has emerged to become a vibrant cultural and tourism center.

processing, alcoholic beverages, tobacco, printing, and electrical goods. It is also a center for medicine, banking, insurance, tourism, and law, and acts as a marketplace for Scottish beef and salmon produce.

GLASGOW is Scotland's largest city has a population of over a quarter million. Shipbuilding and heavy engineering were responsible for its 19th-century prosperity and for its decline due to the world oil crisis in the 1970s. Other industries include textiles, food and beverages, tobacco, chemicals, engineering, and printing. In 1990, it was named a "City of Culture" by the European Community. The famous Glasgow School of Art, the 12th-century cathedral, and the renowned Burrell Collection of art are the major tourist attractions.

CARDIFF [CAERDYDD] The capital city of Wales used to be a major port for exporting coal from nearby mining valleys. Severe reductions in output from the mines and cutbacks in steel production have led to large-scale unemployment. Nevertheless, Cardiff remains a Welsh shopping and service center, home of food processing plants, and light engineering industries. Cardiff Castle, the National Museum of Wales, the National Folk Museum, and the Cardiff Art Gallery are some cultural highlights.

RIVERS

THE THAMES The River Thames rises in the Cotswolds in Gloucestershire and flows out to the North Sea at Tilbury 210 miles to the east. It winds through picturesque scenery until it reaches London. The Thames is used for a variety of boating activities: rowing competitions are regularly held on the river at Henley, Oxford, and Eton; the annual Boat Race on the Thames in London between teams from Oxford and Cambridge Universities is a major highlight.

London's position on the river makes it ideally suited as a port; the Thames below Tower Bridge is an extremely important waterway. Large container ships nowadays dock farther downriver at Tilbury since they cannot pass the Thames Flood Barrier (below) that was built in 1982 to prevent the flooding of London by an unusually high tide. The Dartford Tunnel runs beneath the Thames, and the parallel overhead bridge, complete London's orbital motorway called the M25.

THE RIVER SEVERN The River Severn rises in North Wales and runs through the border country with Wales before reaching the Bristol Channel estuary. Its tidal range can be as much as 40 feet during spring tides. The Severn Bridge over the River Severn just north of Bristol is a major road link between England and Wales, as well as an engineering triumph: built in the 1960s, it spans 3,240 feet.

Winter is generally mild in Britain, but tends to be colder in Scotland and the north and west of Britain.

CLIMATE

Britain enjoys a cool to mild temperate climate with few extremes of temperature. The greatest variation in weather is in the southeast, but throughout Britain, temperatures rarely surpass 90°F in summer or fall below 14°F in winter.

The Gulf Stream, a warm ocean current that crosses the Atlantic Ocean, produces warmer winters in the west of the country so that northwest Scotland is considerably warmer than southeast England in January. Warm and wet Westerly winds prevail, and since most upland areas are in the north and west of the country, it is these regions that have the heaviest rainfall: over 60 inches annually, mainly in the autumn and winter, compared with a national average of 40 inches. September to January are the wettest months, March to June the driest.

Mild winters and high rainfall in the west make this region well suited for livestock farming; by contrast, the sunny summers and the flatter land of the east make it more suited for arable farming. Throughout Britain the weather is always unpredictable, and always a subject for conversation.

FLORA AND FAUNA

Britain enjoys a diverse range of flora and fauna, despite increasing urbanization. Ten national parks in England and Wales conserve different types of rural environments. The uplands boast heather-strewn grouse moors, brackens, and a spiny evergreen shrub known as gorse. Wild roses and hawthorns flourish in southern England; wild daffodils herald spring in Yorkshire and the Lake District, and bluebell woods flourish in the Home Counties. There are 150 different types of grass in the British Isles. The English oak is abundant in forests such as Savernake Forest in Wiltshire and Sherwood Forest in Nottinghamshire; beechwoods are found in the Chilterns, and pine forests abound in Scotland.

Wild deer and ponies are found in Hampshire's New Forest (below); deer are found in some other woods, including areas of the West County, and in the Scottish Highlands. Foxes, otters, bats, badgers, and field mice have adapted to the urban environment and are found throughout Britain. The red robin is a popular and territorial garden bird. Coastal areas and plowed arable land attract seagulls and hawks, while the larger birds of prey stalk highlands and even freeways in search of food. The peregrine falcon and ptarmigan are found in the Scottish Highlands. Gray seals are common in underpopulated coastal areas. Brown trout and grayling are often found in rivers, while salmon and eel spend most of their lives at sea but return to spawn in rivers.

HISTORY

THE HISTORY OF PEOPLE in Britain stretches back for over 5,000 years. A brief outline is given here.

EARLY SETTLERS AND INVADERS

Barrows—communal burial grounds on the chalk uplands of southern England—are remnants of Britain's earliest Neolithic people, who arrived from the Iberian peninsula and North Africa in about 3,000 B.C. The Beaker people (so-called because of their pottery skills) built hill forts, cultivated barley, and were buried in individual graves from around 2,400 B.C.

From 700 B.C., different tribes of Celts arrived from Central Europe, bringing with them the knowledge of ironworking that revolutionized agriculture. They established hill forts and trade outlets on the rivers Thames and Firth of Forth. Their society was stratified and included a caste of Druid priests and a ruling warrior class.

The Romans invaded Britain in A.D. 43 and occupied the south of Britain from the River Humber to the River Severn. They established garrison towns to watch over upland areas they did not control. Boudicca, female leader of the Celts, was unsuccessful in driving the Romans away in A.D. 61. The Romans brought Christianity to Britain but failed to conquer Caledonia (now Scotland); the Emperor Hadrian build a wall from coast to coast in the north of England to prevent incursions of Picts and Scots across the border. The last Roman troops left Britain around A.D. 409.

Above: **A statue of the Celtic leader Boudicca in Colchester.**

Opposite: **The famous and fascinating prehistoric stone circles of Stonehenge. The stones average a height of 13.5 ft. above ground and 4.5 ft. below. Their origin and purpose are unknown.**

Vikings were sea rovers and pirates from present-day Scandinavia. They ravaged the coasts of Europe from the 8th to the 10th centuries.

THE ANGLO-SAXONS

Three Germanic tribes invaded soon after the Romans left. The Angles settled in the east, the Saxons further west and in the north Midlands, and the Jutes in Kent and the South Coast, driving the Celts farther north and west. The Anglo-Saxons founded the different kingdoms of Essex, Sussex, Wessex, Middlesex, East Anglia, Northumbria, and Mercia. Anglo-Saxon kings included King Offa of Mercia (757–796), who built a long dike on the Welsh borders to keep the Celts at bay, and King Alfred of Wessex, called Alfred the Great (871–899), who used educated churchmen to draw up laws and began the record the *Anglo Saxon Chronicle*. Monks from the Scottish island Iona and the Northumbrian island Lindisfarne continued to spread the Christian religion. In the late 6th century, the monk Augustine (?–A.D. 604) became Britain's first Archbishop of Canterbury.

The Vikings from Norway and Denmark conquered and then settled all of England except Wessex in 865. Successors of King Alfred of Wessex drove the Vikings out, but incursions intensified from about 980.

In 843, the Highland tribes of Picts and Scots were united into one kingdom under King Kenneth MacAlpin. The Lowlands of Scotland were inhabited by Britons and Angles from Northumbria. In 934, the Scots were defeated by the Wessex army. Wales was mostly settled by Celts by the 8th century, when family groupings became small kingdoms. Gruffydd ap Llewelyn (1039–1063) was a prominent Welsh leader.

The Anglo-Saxons developed communal strip farming using large plows. A council of wise men—the Witan—issued laws and chose kings.

The history of Britain after Roman times is marked by the names of the succeeding royal houses, e.g., the Normans, Plantagenets, and Tudors.

THE NORMANS

King Edward the Confessor (1042–1066) promised the English throne to Duke William of Normandy, but the Witan chose Harold Godwinson of Wessex instead. Shortly after the Danish Vikings attacked in the north of Britain in 1066 and were defeated by King Harold, Duke William invaded the south and defeated Harold in the Battle of Hastings and claimed the English throne.

King William I—William the Conquerer—saw England as the Crown's personal property. He deprived most Saxon lords of their lands and gave half to Norman nobles, one quarter to the church and kept one fifth for himself. Royal hunting grounds such as the 92,170-acre New Forest in Hampshire date from this time. The *Domesday Book* of 1086 records landholdings and agricultural practices after this redistribution of land.

As Duke of Normandy, William gave nominal allegiance to the King of France. The business of governing Britain was conducted wherever King William and his royal court happened to be, since he traveled constantly.

The Bayeux Tapestry recounts, in more than 60 episodes, the expedition across the English Channel by William the Conqueror and his victory over Harold. In this particular scene, the appearance of Halley's Comet in 1066 is also recorded.

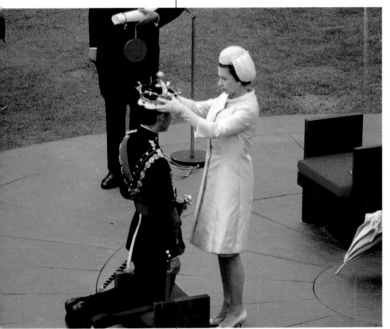

The investiture of the present Prince of Wales in 1969 when he was 21 years old. This age is traditionally considered as the coming of age, or reaching adulthood.

THE PLANTAGENETS

William's death was followed by disputes over the throne. Subsequent monarchs strengthened ties with France by marriage, and even claimed the French throne.

The murder of the Archbishop Thomas à Becket, in Canterbury Cathedral in 1170, was part of the Church-State dispute during the reign of Henry II (1154–1189). Richard I (1189–1199)—Richard the Lionheart—went on several crusades to the Holy Land. His brother, King John, ruled so badly that the nobles forced him to sign the Magna Carta in 1215. The document heralded the start of political rights and personal liberties in Britain. During the reign of his successor Henry III (1216–1272), nobles led by Simon de Montfort formed a council that became Parliament. Edward I (1272–1307) conquered Wales, killing the Welsh leader Llewelyn in 1282 and installing his own son as Prince of Wales in Caernarvon Castle in 1284. He also installed his own nominee on the throne of Scotland, but his successor was defeated by the Scots at the Battle of Bannockburn in 1314.

Further disputes over the succession occurred in the late 14th and early 15th centuries. Edward II (1307–1327) was deposed and murdered. Under Edward III (1327–1377) England entered the Hundred Years War with France that lasted from 1337 to 1453 and resulted in the loss of all English-owned French lands except for Calais. Edward's successor Richard II

(1377–1399) was deposed. Relative stability returned with Henry IV (1399–1413) and Henry V (1413–1422), but under Henry VI (1422–1461), the nobles with armies divided into the houses of Lancaster and York in the Wars of the Roses. When Edward IV (1461–1483), a Yorkist, died in 1483, Richard of Gloucester imprisoned Edward's two sons in the Tower of London where they were murdered, and then declared himself Richard III (1483–1485).

THE TUDORS AND THE EARLY STUARTS

Henry Tudor defeated Richard III at the Battle of Bosworth Field in 1485 to become Henry VII (1485–1509). Although he was a Lancastrian, he

married Elizabeth of York to end the feud. He pacified and tamed the overly powerful Welsh nobles through a powerful court system, and tried to make the English crown financially independent. His son, Henry VIII (1509–1547), involved England in long military campaigns on the European continent. Henry VIII's desire for a male heir led him to marry six times and caused a split between the English Church and papal authority in Rome. Under him, an Act of Union joined Wales to England in 1536. Wales gained representation in Parliament, place names were changed from

Caernarvon Castle in North Wales, the traditional site for the investiture of the Prince of Wales since 1284.

Welsh to English, and the principality was organized into counties. In Scotland, Henry VIII won a victory at Flodden in 1513.

Henry VIII's son, Edward VI (1547–1553), ruled as a minor, during which time the Protestant religion was practiced, but under Edward's stepsister Mary (1553–1558), Protestant preachers were prosecuted and England reverted to Roman Catholicism. Protestantism returned once more with Elizabeth I (1558–1603). During her reign, the Spanish Armada was defeated, America was "discovered," and the arts flourished.

Elizabeth I never married, so the throne passed to her cousin James VI of Scotland, who became James I of England (1603–1625). His accession cemented the two countries together, although this was only finalized a century later with the Act of Union of 1707. Under James, the Authorized Version of the Bible was published in 1611, and the *Mayflower* set off from Plymouth in 1620 to found a new Puritan colony in America.

THE CIVIL WAR AND THE RESTORATION

Both James I and his son Charles I became increasingly dependent on Parliament for money to run their governments. Every time Parliament granted further taxes, it demanded new powers. For instance, the 1628 Petition of Right, granting individual citizens freedom from arbitrary arrest and imprisonment, is one of the most far-reaching results of this period. Charles I further antagonized Parliament by marrying a Roman Catholic.

He also tried to impose Anglican Church practice on the fiercely Puritan Scottish Kirk (church), which led to war with Scotland.

To fight the Scots, Charles had to ask Parliament for more money. In 1642, his attempt to arrest five Members of Parliament in the House of Commons precipitated a civil war. The war between Royalists and Parliamentarians lasted until 1645, when the Royalists were defeated at the Battle of Naseby. The victors drew their support primarily from the navy, merchants, and the City of London. In 1649, Charles I and his wife Henrietta Maria were executed, and England became a Commonwealth under Oliver Cromwell until his death in 1658. Sporadic fighting continued against the Royalists.

By 1660, with no clear sign of a new leader, Charles II (1660–1685), son of the executed monarch, was asked to return to the throne. This period is called the Restoration. The Test Act of 1673 precluded any Catholic from holding public office. Charles II was careful to be accommodating in his reign, but his brother James II tried to overturn anti-Catholic legislation, married a Catholic, and was believed by many to be a Catholic himself.

Above: **Re-enactment of a battle in the Civil War by the Sealed Knot Society, a latter-day society that re-enacts important historical battles.**

Opposite: **Portrait of Elizabeth I.**

THE GLORIOUS REVOLUTION

Parliament invited the Dutch King William, married to Charles II's daughter Mary, to invade in the name of Protestantism, which he did in 1688, forcing James to flee to Ireland. William (1688–1702) and Mary (1688–1694) were offered the crown jointly by Parliament. From that time, Parliament was stronger than the Crown in Britain. In 1689, a Bill of Rights was passed, which guaranteed individual liberties including the freedom of religion. In 1701, an Act of Settlement was adopted that allows only a Protestant to inherit the crown, a law still in force today.

William defeated James II and his Roman Catholic supporters at the Battle of the Boyne in Ireland in 1690, a date still kept alive in Irish memory. Stuart supporters in Scotland rebelled in the early 18th century, which resulted in the Act of Union of 1707. James II's son James started the Jacobite rebellion in Scotland in 1715. James II's grandson, Bonnie Prince Charlie, defeated an English army at Edinburgh in 1745, but was eventually defeated in 1746 at the Battle of Culloden.

After William and Mary, the throne passed to Anne (1702–1714), Charles II's other daughter, and then to George of Hanover, great grandson of James I.

At the end of the War of Spanish Sucession in 1714, Britain was the leading international power, with 12 colonies on the east coast of America, sugar possessions in the West Indies, a flourishing slave trade between Africa and America, and expanding trading interests in India, the Far East and the Pacific.

Economic life expanded. New canals and waterways improved the distribution of goods, and weekly markets were replaced by regularly stocked shops. Agricultural reforms and the fencing in of land led to widespread rural poverty and a mobile labor force—preconditions for the 19th-century industrial revolution.

THE INDUSTRIAL REVOLUTION

An increasing population's demand for clothes, goods, and houses, coupled with growing scientific knowledge and inventions, led to the Industrial Revolution. Instead of doing handwork at home, workers at machines in factories produced large numbers of goods, and Britain became "the workshop of the world."

The textile industry benefited greatly from scientific inventions. James Hargreaves' spinning jenny of the 1760s spun thread on multiple spinning wheels; Richard Arkwright's water frame further refined spinning and harnessed water power successfully, while Samuel Crompton's mule-jenny combined the two. Edmund Cartwright invented a power loom in 1785 that used animal power at first and later, steam power.

Abraham Darby's invention of the coke smelting process in Coalbrookdale in 1709 enabled Britain to use its large natural deposits of iron; Henry Cort invented a "puddling" process for making wrought or malleable iron, as opposed to cast iron. He also invented a rolling mill. John Wilkinson built the first iron bridge across the Severn at Ironbridge, which opened in 1779 (below). In the 1780s, the first iron ship was built, as were cast-iron pipes for city water systems.

The coal industry benefited from scientific inventions, too. In the early 1700s, a steam pump

helped to drain pits. This was refined by James Watt into the steam engine in 1769. Steam power was used for draining and hauling in the coal industry; further improvements in propping, lighting, and ventilation developed during the 19th century. The steam engine was adopted by other manufacturing industries and formed the basis of Stephenson's Rocket, the first steam locomotive, in 1829, which triggered the mid-19th century railway boom. Engineering and machine tool industries also developed.

The growth of new industrial towns such as Manchester, with their own merchant classes, led to major social change and growing political demands. Working conditions in factories and coal pits were highly exploitative, but were gradually improved during the 19th century. Not everyone welcomed the new machinery: old hand weavers attacked the new machines; they became known as Luddites after a mythical leader, Ned Ludd, who led protests against technological innovation in northern England in the 19th century.

THE VICTORIAN AGE

Queen Victoria (1837–1901) presided over a golden age of British expansion, imperialism, and world domination. The two-party system in Parliament evolved in the 1860s, as Benjamin Disraeli and William Gladstone alternated as prime ministers and heads of the Conservative and Liberal governments respectively.

Overseas trade led to numerous foreign entanglements: in 1839, the Opium Wars with China; in the 1840s, a war with Afghanistan; in 1854, the Crimean War against the Russians that is best remembered for the notorious Charge of the Light Brigade and the acclaimed nursing efforts of Florence Nightingale. In 1857, the Indian mutiny briefly called into question the colonial philosophy. Suez in Egypt was invaded in 1882 to protect Britain's shipping route to India. From 1899 to 1902, the Boer War took place in South Africa in a climate of growing competition with other European powers for African colonies, known as the "Scramble for Africa."

In addition to industrial and imperial achievements, the Victorian age was a time of great artistic output. The towering town halls and municipal buildings such as the Albert Memorial and Royal Albert Hall in London summed up the self-confidence of the time.

THE EARLY 20TH CENTURY

The age of King Edward VII (1902–1910) was increasingly overshadowed by a growing European military build-up and the onset of World War I in 1914. Atrocious casualties in trench warfare were suffered at the Battle of the Somme (France) in 1916, and at Passchendale (Belgium) in 1917. There were over one million British casualties in World War I.

The suffragette movement for women's political rights gained momentum in the prewar years. During the war, women took the places of fighting men in armaments factories and agriculture, and at the end of the war in 1918, women over the age of 30 gained the vote for the first time.

Home rule had been agreed for Ireland just before the outbreak of the war. A bloody Irish uprising during Easter in 1916 was suppressed harshly by English troops. In 1921, the Anglo-Irish Treaty, which divided the Roman Catholic south from the Protestant north, was signed.

During the 1920s, Britain experienced a severe economic depression and high unemployment. Unrest in the coal industry led to the General

Above: **World War I trench warfare on the western front (France) in 1915.**

Opposite: **The Victorian architecture of the town hall in Manchester.**

Edward VIII and Wallis Simpson living as ordinary citizens in the United States. This picture was taken in 1957.

Strike of 1926, when workers from all industries stopped working for a week. The world economic crisis hit Britain hard during the 1930s, with the industrial heartlands of South Wales, the Midlands, and the north of England particularly affected.

In 1936, a royal crisis shook the nation as Edward VIII abdicated in order to marry Wallis Simpson, a divorced woman. His brother became King George VI (1936–1952). George's widow Elizabeth is today's beloved Queen Mother.

From 1937 onward, the armaments industry revived as Britain prepared for the war against Germany that broke out in 1939. As prime minister, Winston Churchill became a revered and respected wartime leader. Civilian casualties were numerous from German bombing raids in England, and battles against the Germans, Italians, and the Japanese were fought in Europe, Africa, and the Far East. The Allied victory in Europe in 1945 was ensured by American involvement in the war effort. Victory over Japan that year was hastened by the use of the atomic bomb.

POSTWAR BRITAIN

In the 1940s and 1950s, there were food shortages and rationing in Britain, as well as large-scale reconstruction. Social measures passed during these years form the basis of today's welfare system: the National Health Service was established, state education was provided for all, and steps towards reducing unemployment and protecting pensions were introduced.

Gradually, the former colonies gained their independence from Britain. The formation of the Commonwealth partly compensated Britain for the economic consequences of this as the Commonwealth member countries were overseas markets for Britain's goods. In 1973, Britain joined the European Community (EC).

Politics developed largely into a two-party Labour and Conservative seesaw. The oil crisis of 1973 rocked the economy, and increasing union demands against a backdrop of unemployment brought down the Labour government in 1979, and brought to power the Conservative Party led by Margaret Thatcher. During the 1980s, the southeast of England experienced a boom, while the economies of the industrial areas continued to contract. The current world recession has pushed unemployment levels still higher.

Former prime minister Margaret Thatcher, now Lady Thatcher, was one of Britain's most dynamic and controversial leaders. She won three successive elections and held office from 1979 to 1990, when she was ousted from the leadership by her own party in their attempt to gain electoral support.

GOVERNMENT

THE UNITED KINGDOM of Great Britain and Northern Ireland is a constitutional monarchy. The monarch has a predominantly ceremonial role as head of state, whose duties include the formal appointment of the prime minister, accepting the resignations of prime ministers before elections, and opening Parliament each year. He or she also meets each week with the prime minister to discuss current issues and carries out a diplomatic role by receiving and entertaining foreign heads of state.

Above: **Flags on some of the buildings in Whitehall, the district of London where Britain's government offices are situated.**

Opposite: **Big Ben, the famous clock at the eastern wing of the Houses of Parliament.**

The government works on a system of parliamentary democracy. Elections are held at least every five years. All citizens on the electoral roll over the age of 18 can vote, although it is not compulsory to do so. The political party that wins a majority of seats in Parliament forms a government, in alliance with other parties if necessary to form a majority.

The day-to-day business of government is decided by a cabinet of up to 20 ministers chosen by the prime minister. This cabinet includes the Chancellor of the Exchequer—the minister who presents the annual budget on the country's finances—and ministers representing the different government departments such as the Home Office (domestic affairs), the Foreign Office, Health, Education, and Trade and Industry.

PARLIAMENT

The United Kingdom has a two-tier parliamentary system. Bills are debated and passed first in the House of Commons, or lower house, which has 650 elected Members of Parliament (MPs). The MPs represent the 523 English, 38 Welsh, 72 Scottish, and 17 Northern Irish constituencies, each of which contains approximately 60,000 voters. MPs have been paid salaries since 1963.

Proceedings in the House of Commons are run by the Speaker, who calls on different speakers in turn, and keeps order in the sometimes unruly debates. Parliamentary debates are televised, reported on the radio, and recorded verbatim in a publication called *Hansard*. Parliamentary committees are formed to investigate policies, with members from different political parties taking part. The Public Accounts Committee, for example, questions the government's spending policies.

The House of Lords, or upper house, is not a representative body. It is comprised of the Lords Spiritual (the two archbishops and other bishops) and the Lords Temporal (those who have

inherited titles, also known as the aristocracy, other peers appointed for life as a recognition of their public service and good deeds; and the Law Lords, those at the head of the legal system.) Only a small proportion of those entitled to do so regularly attend the parliamentary proceedings. The House of Lords debates those bills that have passed the House of Commons, and its role is generally to give assent to their passage, although it has occasionally succeeded in opposing governments on specific policies. Debate is more leisurely and gentlemanly than in the House of Commons.

Once bills have passed through both the House of Commons and the House of Lords, the monarch gives Royal Assent to them before they become law.

The best future for Britain. [graffiti: WORST; conservative X; VOTE LABOUR]

MAIN POLITICAL PARTIES

Since World War II, the government of Britain has been split between the two main political parties, the Conservative Party and the Labour Party.

The Conservative Party is largely committed to encouraging business through lower direct taxes and strict controls on inflation by limiting government spending. It pursues a "hands-off" policy, leaving companies to stand alone rather than investing in supportive infrastructure. Its main support is in the wealthier areas of Britain, where people earn enough to benefit from lower taxes and do not depend on dwindling welfare payments.

The Labour Party has historically held socialist values, championing the worker, as opposed to the employer, with support from the various trade unions. It concentrates on such matters as working conditions and sees a more active role for government in supporting industrial enterprises that generate wealth and employment. The Labour Party nationalized (took into government ownership) vital industries such as coal, electricity, water, and the postal and telecommunications industries, while the Conservative Party has recently privatized these vital industries.

Above: **Speaker's Corner in Hyde Park, London, is a place where people air their views. Anyone can speak, and it is usually done on Sundays when there are more people in the park. Freedom of speech is a fundamental right in Britain.**

Opposite: **IRA bomb damage in downtown Manchester.**

OTHER POLITICAL PARTIES

The Liberal Democratic Party is the third main political party, occupying the central political ground between the Conservative and Labour parties. The Liberals, formerly called the Whigs, have suffered diminishing support since World War II. During the 1970s, the Liberals allied with the Labour Party, and in the 1980s allied with a new party, the Social Democrats, which splintered from the Labour Party before the 1983 election. Initially the new alliance did well in the polls, but unclear direction and disputes between the two elements led to a split and a further dilution of support.

The Greens, formerly the Ecology Party, enjoy small but growing support for their environmental policies. Their main achievement has been in introducing environmental policies to the major political parties. The Greens domestic and foreign policies are less specific or clear.

REGIONAL PARTIES AND POLITICS

Plaid Cymru ("Ply-d Kum-ree"), the Welsh nationalist party, which was founded in 1925, became very active during the 1970s. It generally gains a large proportion of Welsh seats, and has done much for the Welsh. For example, Wales gained its own television and radio channels, the Welsh language was reintroduced to schools in the 1970s, and all road signs and government publications are printed in both Welsh and English. Plaid Cymru supports Welsh devolution from Britain. However, in the 1979 referendum, only 11.8% Welsh people voted for devolution from the United Kingdom.

The Scottish National Party (SNP) wins a high proportion of the vote in Scottish politics. The SNP is in favor of devolution from the United Kingdom, and claims the revenue from the North Sea oil for Scotland. A referendum was held in 1979 but the turnout of voters was insufficient to support the move for devolution. Scotland has its own legal and education systems, and its own banknotes, which are issued by Scottish banks supported by the Bank of England. Scottish pounds are valued exactly the same as English pounds, and the currencies are interchangeable.

Two Northern Irish parties, the Ulster Unionists, representing the Protestant cause in Northern Ireland, and the Social Democratic and Labour Party (SDLP), representing mainstream Catholics, have MPs in Parliament. Sinn Fein, the political wing of the Irish Republican Army (IRA), has elected MPs, but they have refused to take their seats in Parliament. Terrorist activities by extremist Catholic and Protestant groups in Northern Ireland are regular occurrences in Northern Ireland and sporadic IRA campaigns also take place on the British mainland.

The Channel Islands and the Isle of Man are both self-governing in most aspects of domestic policy.

The central Criminal Court in London, better known as the Old Bailey, is the leading criminal court. The sword and scales represent truth and justice.

LOCAL GOVERNMENT

England is divided into 39 non-metropolitan counties, 36 metropolitan districts, and 32 Greater London boroughs. Each has its own council. Wales is divided into county councils and district councils, and Scotland has regional, island, and district councils. Each local government authority is responsible for its council's spending on matters such as education, law enforcement, road repairs, housing, health care, and promoting the arts. Inner city areas often incur higher costs than rural areas in order to supply sufficient services to their larger populations.

THE LEGAL SYSTEM

Uniquely, Britain does not have a written constitution. Instead it relies on a large body of precedent cases or "common law," built up since the 11th century. In addition to this body of law, there is legislation passed by

THE POLICE

Britain does not have a single national police force, instead it has different independent police forces corresponding to regional areas. England and Wales have 41 police forces, as well as two for London—the Metropolitan Police (right) and the City of London Police. Scotland has another eight units. The United Kingdom has a total of 147,000 policemen and policewomen, roughly one officer to every 400 citizens. Police officers of different forces frequently co-operate on crime cases. Other than for specific cases such as anti-terrorist work, or when tackling armed robbery, the police in Britain do not carry firearms, and to do so requires authorization for each particular case.

Parliament, known as statute law, and law passed by the European Community, which in many cases takes precedence over British domestic law. There are three elements to the legal system in the United Kingdom: that of England and Wales, Scotland, and Northern Ireland.

In England and Wales, 95% of criminal cases are tried first in magistrates' or local courts, which can recommend sentences not exceeding a $3,000 fine or 6 months in prison. Some large cities also have magistrates paid by the state as full-time judicial officers, who sit alone and decide cases. More serious cases are referred to the crown courts. There are 90 of these in England and Wales, presided over by a judge, with a jury of 12 citizens to assess guilt and pass sentences. The Central Criminal Court in London, known as the Old Bailey, is the ultimate criminal court; the Royal Courts of Justice, in the Strand in London, is the ultimate civil court. A system of legal aid (government funding for taking action in the courts) is available for victims of crimes and for criminal defendants, but is not available for civil cases.

In Scotland, most minor criminal cases are tried informally in police courts in the towns and in magistrates' courts in the countryside. More serious criminal cases are tried in the sheriff courts, where the sheriff sits alone for minor cases and with a jury for more serious cases.

The Metropolitan Police force of 3,000 paid constables was established in 1829 by Sir Robert Peel, the home secretary at the time. The nickname "Bobby" comes from him.

ECONOMY

BRITAIN JOINED the Economic Community (EC) in 1973 to be part of the united market for European manufactured and agricultural goods. Together with the United States, Japan, Canada, Germany, France, and Italy, Britain is one of the seven leading industrial nations (G7) in the world. However, Britain is currently suffering its worst economic recession since World War II. Much of its economy is in decline, especially heavy industries that were built around the coalfields—steel, iron, engineering, and chemicals.

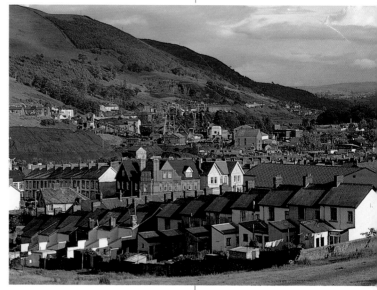

INDUSTRY

Britain's heavy manufacturing industry originally developed nearby sources of power. For example, heavy engineering, steel production, manufacturing for the oil industry, shipbuilding, and ship repair facilities all developed near the Northumberland and Durham coalfields. In nearby Teeside, a chemical industry developed to turn coal by-products, chemicals from the Tees salt field, and oil refinery by-products into paints, fertilizers, explosives, plastics, and textiles. Chemical industries also developed along Merseyside near Liverpool. Steel production boomed in South Wales and Sheffield, and both have adjacent coalfields.

In the Midlands, Coventry was a boomtown during the heyday of the car industry in the 1950s, generating spinoff industrial activity for motor parts and other consumer goods. Cars from the United States and the United Kingdom dominated world markets during the 1950s, but were

Above: **A mining town in South Wales. Mining communities like these are becoming scarce due to government closure of mines over the last decade.**

Opposite: **A view of the dock area of Felixstowe in Suffolk on the eastern coast of England. Felixstowe is both a container port and a passenger ferry link with Belgium, Holland, Norway, and Sweden.**

Canary Wharf, located in an area of former docks and shipping wharves, was developed in the 1980s as an extension of the financial center of the City of London. Unfortunately, the completion of the Canary Wharf project coincided with a real estate crash and the current recession. Very few offices are currently occupied but this may change with the new subway link from central London.

overtaken by West Germany, France, Italy, and increasingly Japan; in 1986 the British company Austin Rover started making cars for the Japanese firm Honda.

The pharmaceuticals industry grew rapidly during the 1980s, exporting 34% of its output in 1984, but its research and development costs remain high. The synthetic fiber industry grew in the 1960s, but dropped off during the 1970s.

Some old industrial areas in the northeast, northwest, and the Midlands are now benefiting from Japanese investment in industrial expansion zones. These zones allow investors to benefit from tax incentives as well as using Britain as a springboard into the EC market. Car production, light electrical goods manufacture, and the production of high technology equipment are representative industries.

The corridor alongside the M4 freeway linking London to South Wales has attracted high technology industries. The easy access to markets and airports, and an attractive working environment combined with a pool of highly-trained personnel, have led to a prospering computer industry, with computer software tailored for the individual, business, finances and defense. High-quality audio goods, again requiring innovative technical skills, also enjoy some success in these new industrial areas.

SOURCES OF ENERGY

Britain's coal reserves are the largest in the European Community, but most deep-face coal mines in the northeast, the Midlands, and South Wales are now considered too expensive to exploit. Many pits have recently been closed, severely affecting local communities as many people have lost their jobs. The electric companies are major customers for coal, with coal-fired power stations located along the River Thames and the Trent Valley. Since their privatization, the electric companies have been buying cheaper imported coal.

In the 1970s oil was discovered in the North Sea. Profitable fields lie to the east of mainland Scotland near the Orkney Islands. Sullom Voe on the Shetland Islands, Scapa Flow on the Orkney Islands, and Aberdeen on the mainland have all become important oil and gas ports, with oil-fired power stations located nearby. In 1988, North Sea oil and gas accounted for 5% of the United Kingdom's Gross National Product (GNP), but this is unlikely to continue as some reserves are already running low. Scotland and part of Northumbria have some hydroelectric power, due to the high rainfall in these areas. In Kinlochleven, Scotland, hydroelectric power is used to smelt aluminum. Nuclear power stations are located in remote coastal areas of Scotland, the northwest (below), along the south coast, East Anglia, and the Bristol Channel. Eighteen percent of Britain's electricity is generated from nuclear power while the rest is from fossil fuels such as coal.

Above: **Traffic congestion is a frequent occurrence in the major cities. Inner-city traffic congestion is a growing problem: traffic in Inner London is reported to travel no faster now than in the 1920s, at roughly 8 miles an hour.**

Opposite: **The Bank of England in central London.**

INFRASTRUCTURE

Britain's network of roads emanates outward from London to reach the rest of the country. The major freeways, generally three lanes in each direction, are frequently clogged with excess traffic.

Frequent labor unrest in the past and an unreliable train service resulted in much freight being transported by truck. Passenger rail fares have become some of the most expensive in Europe. British Rail, still under government ownership, is targeted for privatization. The Channel Tunnel, due for completion in 1994, will provide a 31-mile rail link from Folkestone, England, to Coquelles, France, as part of a London to Paris link.

The London Underground system has 254 miles of railway track, but it is a struggle to satisfy the ever-increasing consumer demand. At peak hours, trains are frequently overcrowded, and bomb scares often disrupt train timetables. Buses are a crucial component of the public transportation system throughout Britain.

Seventy-seven percent of Britain's trade is carried by sea from 300 ports: those on the west coast, such as Liverpool, Bristol, and Clydeside, are well-sited for trade across the Atlantic. Now that Britain's trade is predominantly with the EC, ports on the east coast such as Felixstowe, and Channel ports such as Dover have become more important.

THE SERVICE SECTOR

In 1987, 67.8% of economically active workers were employed in the service sector. Retailing and distribution is the third largest sector of the U.K. economy. Retail trade remains fairly busy, although people spend less on consumer goods during a recession. The public service sector is a major sector in the economy, employing more than four million people in the various government departments such as social services, health, the Treasury, education, and the Home Office.

Real estate was booming in the 1980s as many people bought homes with easily available mortgages. This sector is now in decline as house and office prices fell drastically due to excessive supply. This, in turn, has caused a decline in the construction industry.

Many tourists take advantage of the British pound's comparatively favorable exchange rate. Tourism has contributed to the hotel, catering, and retail industries.

BANKING AND FINANCE

London is one of the world's leading financial and banking centers; offices of all major banks and institutions are located in or near the square mile of the City. The financial sector has also been hit by the current recession, and people working in banks, brokerage houses, and other financial institutions have lost their jobs. Shares are traded electronically rather than on the floor of the Stock Exchange. The Bank of England is the government's banker and prints banknotes; it has considerable freedom in its daily operations, and attempts to regulate currency values.

AGRICULTURE

Seventy-seven percent of Britain's land area is used for agriculture, but this sector only employs 2.3% of the workforce. The main agricultural output is from dairy and cattle farming.

Britain's agricultural produce is determined by climate and geography. The highland west of the island, with its high rainfall, is well suited for pasture farming: sheep are raised in the Scottish Highlands, in Wales, and in Cornwall. By contrast, the flatter, drier land on the east is better suited for arable farming; the fenland of East Anglia and Cambridgeshire is particularly fertile. Large-scale farms, ideal for large combine harvesters, are highly profitable. Horticulture is practiced in Kent and the Vale of Evesham, and fishing and salmon farming are important in Scotland and along the coasts.

Britain's agricultural trade is now governed by the EC, whose Common Agricultural Policy (CAP) subsidizes the poorer farmers of the community and imposes quotas on agricultural output. Unfortunately, the quota system penalizes Britain's relatively efficient agricultural sector.

INDUSTRIAL RELATIONS

Britain has 350 trade unions and professional associations, and 140 employers' associations. In times of full employment, trade unions have had the power to negotiate better working conditions, terms of employment, and wages for their members. Their powers were severely curtailed during the 1980s, when a number of laws were passed limiting their power to take industrial action and increasing the rights of non-union members.

With or without unions, employees in Britain have certain legal rights, many of which are aimed at dispelling discrimination—whether on grounds of sex, race, or age. Britain has not subscribed to EC initiatives to standardize minimum wage levels and maximum working hours because it wants to maintain a flexible workforce for its industries.

In 1993, over 10% of Britain's workforce was unemployed; most of the unemployed relied on a complex system of state benefits, calculated on the number of years of employment before the job loss. This high proportion of benefit recipients, along with the increasing number of pensioners also drawing state benefits, have had the effect of increasing government spending and thus the tax demands on the dwindling number of employed people.

THE BRITISH

THE BRITISH ARE inordinately proud of their sense of humor, which is often dry and subtle. Southerners are not particularly talkative, but those in rural communities and further north are more open and always greet strangers. The English love of animals and their propensity to form orderly lines at all times cause great amusement to their Continental neighbors.

Stereotypes about the Scottish include their reputation for dourness and stinginess; the Welsh have been labeled by some to be long-winded and to love singing. All such stereotypes are unrepresentative of most individuals.

THE EARLIEST SETTLERS

Some of the people Cornwall, Wales, and western Scotland can trace their ancestry back to the Celtic tribes who were driven to these areas over 10 centuries ago.

Angles, Saxons, and Vikings have all left their mark on a basic Celto-Roman gene pool, added to by the invading Normans in 1066. Different waves of immigration from the European continent over the centuries have also added to the British mixture: weavers from Flanders, Huguenots (Protestants) who were expelled from France by Louis XIV, refugees fleeing from continental wars during the 16th and 17th centuries, and French nobles fleeing the extremes of the French Revolution in the 18th century are examples.

Above and opposite: **Some of the many different faces of the British.**

51

DRESS

The British dress similarly to people in other Westernized nations. The cold, damp winters require heavy coats or mackintoshes (raincoats), warm woolens, occasionally even "long johns"—long woolen underwear. The moment the sun comes out, the British quest for a suntan begins, and pale flesh is exposed to the weak sun on beaches, in back gardens, and in public parks.

One of the best-known local traditional dress variations is the Scottish tartan, traditionally made into a kilt. Each Scottish clan has its own tartan, and no one lacking ancestral links to a clan should wear its tartan. In full Highland dress, men wear kilts made of pleated and patterned thick woven woolen material held together with a large safety pin, an ornamental pouch or sporran over the kilt, a tweed jacket, a flat cap with a central pompon (only worn outside), and long socks with a knife inside one sock. In Highland dress, the women wear long tartan skirts, white blouses, and tartan sashes.

Examples of Welsh national dress can be seen at the annual eisteddfods, and regional variations at local summer shows.

The word tartan first appeared in the 15th century, but the Romans referred to their enemies, the Caledonians [Scots], as "wearing chequered garments."

MORE RECENT IMMIGRANT RACES

Britain's Jewish community dates from the 18th century. A large proportion of the major merchant banks and stockbrokerage houses were founded by Jewish families; numerous patrons of the arts, theater producers, politicians, and community leaders also come from the Jewish community. Jews from Central Europe, Hungary, Poland, and Russia also arrived during the 19th century, and from Nazi Germany in the 20th century. One third of all British Jews now live in northwest London, with a sixth of the total Jewish population living in the London borough of Barnet. Manchester also has a significant Jewish population.

Britain enticed laborers from her colonies to help in the postwar reconstruction at home. The *S.S. Empire Windrush* carried the first skilled and semiskilled West Indian workers in 1948. Immigration from the Caribbean colonies increased from 11,000 in 1954 to 34,000 in 1962, after

the United States introduced immigration controls in the early 1950s. The majority of Britain's West Indian population settled in Greater London, mainly in Clapham, Brixton, Paddington, and Notting Hill.

Thousands of Asian immigrants from India, Pakistan, and Bangladesh arrived in the 1950s, settling in Greater London and in the manufacturing towns of Birmingham, Leicester, and Bradford, where labor shortages were acute. Ugandan president Idi Amin's expulsion of Asians in 1972 drove 27,000 highly trained and talented Asians of Pakistani descent to migrate to Britain, where many became doctors and professionals.

A community of approximately 125,000 Chinese, mainly from Hong Kong, have also set up small businesses and entered the professions. London has a Chinatown, and most towns throughout England now have Chinese take-out restaurants. Vietnamese boat people fleeing from their Communist government were initially accepted in the early 1980s, but increasingly, immigration controls have been tightened.

With 930 people per square mile, England is the second most densely-populated country in Europe after the Netherlands. Successive immigration and nationality acts now make it hard to gain the right to migrate to Britain.

Many South Asian immigrants have set up general stores in Britain's towns and cities.

ENGLISH SURNAMES

Many British surnames originated several centuries ago and often give clues about early ancestors. Here are some examples.

• Names of nearby places, generally towns—London, Ashby, Baldock. Some French place names appear as surnames—Beecham (Beauchamps), Manners (Meunières). Fleming (from Flanders), and Bremner (from Brabant) also reflect places of origin.

• Names of landscape features—Hill, Brooks, Bridges. Surnames such as Atlee, Townsend, Noakes, and Nash form part of this group, as they combine prepositions (at, end) with the geographical feature.

• Personal names—Peter, William, Donald—and their sons—Peterson, Williamson, and Donaldson. In Scotland the prepositions Fitz and Mac mean "son of," as in FitzWilliam, MacIntosh (Fitz has also been used as a surname for illegitimate royal children—Fitzroy, a rendering of the French word "roi" meaning "king").

In Wales "Ap" shortened to "P" also means "son of"—Prichard (son of Richard), Pugh (son of Hugh), and Powell (son of Howell).

• Names of occupations, trades, offices, or status—Cooper, Weaver, King, and Bishop. Regional variations for the same occupation occur, so that the surnames Tucker, Fuller, and Walker are all surnames from the same process of fulling, or cleaning cloth.

• Names from nicknames, expressions, and animals—Long, Black, Cruikshank (crooked leg), Goodenough, Gough (red-haired), Fox, Herring.

• Relationships—Cousins, Fodder, Vaughan (younger).

RACIAL DISCRIMINATION AND INTEGRATION

There are strict laws regarding employment and civil equality in Britain: it is illegal to advertise job vacancies on the basis of color, creed, or sex, and the Commission for Racial Equality (CRE) has powers to fine offending employers and award damages to those suffering discrimination. In 1993, Britain had four non-white MPs, although in trade unions and numerous other social and economic levels, minorities remain underrepresented. The various races are now better represented at the local council level than previously.

Helping the police. Efforts are being made to improve race relations between the police and minority communities.

Intolerance of immigrants and support for extremist right-wing organizations has been strongest in the poorer inner-city areas such as the east end of London, where Asians are perceived as undercutting pay rates. Immigration officials, customs officials, and police officers seem to detain a disproportionate number of non-white people for questioning, and a few notorious civil cases have shown alarming prejudice among some police forces. During the hot summers of the early 1980s, arrests in black, inner-city ghettoes sparked off riots by disaffected youths in Liverpool, Manchester, and south London. Attempts are being made on a local level to reverse the trend of underachievement in schools and high unemployment among Afro-Caribbeans in particular.

The cheapest housing, provided by local concils, is often run down and unpleasant to live in. Graffiti and vandalism are frequent in common areas such as hallways and entrance halls.

CLASS

Distinctions of accent, topics of conversation and terms used, upbringing, table manners, dress, general deportment, meal times, and preferences for food, drink, and entertainment—all these are clues by which one British person can size up another. Far more complex than the division between blue-collar and white-collar workers, between the employed and the unemployed, is a selection of signals baffling to the outsider but deeply important to the insider in determining another's class and place in society.

At the top of the ladder—apart from the monarchy—is the aristocracy, who have a dwindling economic power, but who enjoy tremendous vestigial influence and respect. Five royal dukes, 24 other dukes, 35 marquesses, 204 earls, and 127 viscounts and barons head a list of about 900 hereditary peers and 1,200 baronets; all pass titles and landed estates to their offspring when they die. A paternalist outlook, a sense of guardianship of property, and a duty to perform public service are widespread attributes of this class. Twice a year, life peers are created by the monarch from all walks of life, in recognition of their contribution to their field or profession.

The middle classes aspire to move up the social ladder. There are numerous subtle gradations within the middle class. The upper middle classes may have earned money in the professions, but the majority generally inherited sufficient wealth to have benefited from the best education, and they aspire to the aristocratic lifestyle by investing in land. The higher echelons of political and economic power and all walks of public life are still dominated by those who attended one of Britain's exclusive "public" schools—

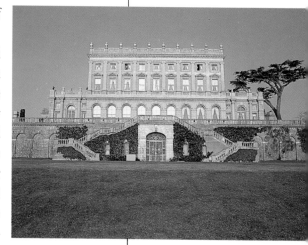

Eton in particular—and either Oxford or Cambridge University. With this continued status quo, it is not surprising that many members of the middle class strive to afford these educational advantages for their own children.

Advertisers group people into social groups A to E: "A" roughly corresponds to the aristocracy or upper class and "B" to the upper middle class of professionals. The advertisers concentrate most of their efforts on the "C" and "D" groups, to which most of the population belong. It is here that the aspirations to climb the social ladder are at their highest.

Non-white immigrant groups stand apart from the class system: in as much as they belong, they are primarily judged to belong to the lower ranks. White foreigners, whether immigrants or just visitors, cannot beas easily spotted as can be the English by their host of subtle signals only they understand. Thus these foreigners remain outsiders.

Late 20th-century Britain remains a divided and economically unequal society, with the top 1% of the population owning over 20% of its wealth. The number of millionaires doubled from 9,000 in 1980 to 18,000 in 1986, while over 10% of the workforce was registered as unemployed.

Cliveden House in Buckinghamshire. Stately homes situated within estates of farmland were the traditional homes of the landed aristocracy. Nowadays, very few can afford the upkeep and estate duties. Many of these stately homes are now open to the public as museums, or have been converted to use as schools or sanitariums.

LIFESTYLE

ECONOMIC CONSIDERATIONS largely determine the lifestyles of different British people. Those who work can afford better homes, education, and leisure pursuits. The increasing number of unemployed people have more limited options, as do pensioners and those on lower incomes. There are great differences between urban and rural lifestyles as there are between the different regions of the country and the different ethnic communities.

In general, the British have small nuclear families consisting of two parents and one or two children. In common with other industrialized countries, the birth rate in Britain is declining. Many aspects of British life are similar to those in other Westernized countries.

FAMILY LIFE

The majority of families have married parents, although an increasing number of people are cohabiting and raising children out of wedlock. In 1983, 23% of live births were to unmarried parents, of which two-thirds were registered by both parents. Those who do choose marriage are marrying later—26 is the average age for men and 24 for women. The age of marriage is younger for manual workers than for the better educated.

Above: **A family outing at a local agricultural fair.**

Opposite: **Gypsy children posing in front of their caravan. Britain has roughly 80,000 traveling gypsies, living in shanty shacks or caravans on the outskirts of towns. Their traditional occupations include working in fairgrounds and traveling circuses, and trading in scrap metal; several also make a living as clairvoyants, or psychics.**

It has become quite common in urban areas for young couples to live together or cohabit before embarking on marriage. In 1983, there were approximately one million single-parent families, and roughly 90% of these single parents were women.

Family size and structure vary between the different immigrant communities. The West Indian community has a comparatively high proportion of single parents: marriage often occurs after the children, who sometimes have different fathers, are born. The South Asian population of over one million, half of which were born in Britain, have traditionally conservative family structures and large kinship networks of support. Often the family is an economic unit, as exemplified in the numerous small grocery stores or restaurants run by Asians. The comparatively small Chinese community is self-reliant, with a generally conservative family structure.

The divorce rate in Britain is high: approximately one in three marriages end in divorce. It is possible to divorce for a number of legal reasons.

In urban areas it is common for both parents to work once the children are in school. Childcare is costly and often difficult to arrange. Women

MARRIAGE

Both parties must be over 16 to marry. If they are under 18, they need parental consent. Every town has a registry office, and all that is required is two witnesses at the ceremony.

Many people marry in religious ceremonies. The Church of England has the authority to solemnize marriages. Members of other denominations and religions are required to have a state registrar present or else to marry in a registry office before the ceremony.

make up nearly half the national workforce. Despite legislation to the contrary, a working woman's average weekly wage is approximately 70% of the working man's average weekly salary. Within families where the wife does not work or earns a lesser amount, it is fairly common for the husband to hand over most of his weekly earnings to his wife, who is generally in charge of the household expenses.

Having parties is a typical way of celebrating children's birthdays, though it can be expensive. Games and birthday cakes are a must.

CHILDHOOD

Most babies are born in hospitals or maternity homes, although it is becoming popular to give birth at home. Childcare remains predominantly the woman's concern, but there are occasional male houseparents when the woman's career is more lucrative than her partner's.

Most children celebrate birthdays, sometimes with costly afternoon parties and games and cakes. The British, particularly the English, still abide by the maxim that children should be seen and not heard, and rarely approve of young children in restaurants or "adult" leisure locations.

Adolescents often express a certain discontent through a youth culture of music, dress styles, and language. Young people with time on their hands often hang around in public places such as shopping centers and public parks, or join youth clubs and use leisure facilities when they can afford to do so. They often want or need some financial independence from their parents. However, this is increasingly difficult as jobs are scarce, particularly for the inexperienced and unskilled. Many have come to rely on social welfare payments.

EDUCATION

Education is free and compulsory for all children between the ages of 6 and 16. In England and Wales, schools are divided into primary (age 6–

11) and secondary (age 11–16) schools, with a national curriculum having achievement tests at the ages of 7, 11, 14, and 16. The major examinations are the GCSE (General Certificate of Secondary Education) taken at age 15 or 16, and the Advanced ("A") Level Exam at age 17 or 18. Nursery schools, run by local education authorities or private foundations, teach those below the age of 5 or 6.

In addition to state schools, there are privately run fee-paying schools (called, confusingly, public schools), where pupils benefit from small classes and a competitive system geared towards university entrance. It is often possible to "board" at such schools, living away from one's parents. These public schools often have more funds than the state schools for extracurricular activities such as sports, drama, and music. Some religious groups such as churches, mosques, and synagogues also run schools, with an emphasis on their religion's moral values and teachings. A total of 7.6% of all children in Britain attend the 2,500 independent schools.

In Scotland, children take the Scottish Certificate of Education at age 16,

which is equivalent to the English GCSE. A year later they take the Highers Examinations in a number of subjects. If they remain in school until age 18, they can take the Sixth Year Studies exams, equivalent to England's "A" (advanced) levels.

The school day is typically from 9 a.m. to 4 p.m., with three academic terms—autumn, spring, and summer—and a long summer vacation between mid-July and early September.

Entrance to one of Britain's universities, including the independent University of Buckingham and the Open University, is attained by competitive entry through "A" level examinations or equivalent.

Thirty polytechnics offer more technical courses and prepare adult students for academic examinations, while more specialized colleges such as the Royal College of Art provide expert instruction to pupils. Unfortunately, many graduates of technical colleges and universities today are graduating with little prospect of employment.

OLD AGE

Grandparents often live apart from their children and grandchildren because of the expense of housing or the need for families to travel to other parts of Britain to find employment. Retirement homes, private or state-funded, provide basic care for those too frail to look after themselves. It is common for families to place elderly relatives in such homes rather than care for them at home.

Pensions are often insufficient to pay for proper food and heat. Every cold winter, the media features distressing stories of elderly people unable or unwilling to spend enough money on fuel to keep warm.

Above: Two older women enjoying a walk in Green Park in central London.

Opposite: Graduation day at Cambridge University.

HEALTHCARE

Basic healthcare is provided free of charge by the National Health Service, funded with tax revenues by the central government. The service, with its rising costs and rising expectations, is a constant subject of political debate.

Doctors' surgeries are found in all local communities. If a person is very sick, a doctor will make a housecall. There is approximately one doctor for every 2,000 persons.

Patients are referred to hospitals by doctors, although there is an acute shortage of hospital beds. Junior doctors and nurses in hospitals often work extremely long hours, with little or no sleep between shifts.

SOCIAL WELFARE

There are a number of welfare benefits available to the most needy members of the community, funded partly by the state, partly by employers, and partly by an indirect tax, called National Insurance, paid by employees and the self-employed. Sickness benefits, unemployment benefits, state pensions, widows' pensions, and maternity pay are all funded this way. An estimated eight million people, many unemployed and single parents, receive Income Support that covers basic living costs, medical prescriptions, dental care, and school meals. Family Credit is available to help those on low incomes. Housing Benefit covers the cost of basic rented housing, while Child Benefit is payable to all mothers regardless of their incomes, until their children reach the age of 18.

Social security payments account for almost one third of all government spending. With an increase in the number of people retiring each year, this spending is set to escalate.

HOUSING

There is a wide range of housing in Britain, from the idyllic country cottage to different types of apartments in the larger cities. Over 80% of Britain's population live in houses or bungalows, the remainder in apartments. Of Britain's 22 million domestic dwellings in 1992, 67% were owner-occupied, 8% were rented out by landlords or housing associations, and 25% were in the public sector.

During the 1980s people were encouraged to buy their own homes, and

from 1979 to 1991 there was a 10% increase in home ownership. Ownership was financed by mortgages, but in the early 1990s, a number of homes were repossessed by the savings and loans societies and mortgage companies as interest rates increased, the recession deepened, and people lost their jobs.

Some of the most reasonably-priced rental housing used to be provided by local councils to the most needy in their areas. In 1980, the government allowed tenants to buy their own council house or apartment. As the sale of this rental property was not accompanied by a building program, the housing available at the cheaper end of the rental market decreased dramatically. As a result, some inner-city councils found that they had to house needy families in costly bed-and-breakfast accommodation instead of proper homes.

A distressing by-product of the 1980s, evident to any visitor to London or other major cities, is the number of homeless people living on the streets, often with only a cardboard box for shelter.

Above: **An increasing number of people are becoming homeless and living on the streets, particularly in the larger cities.**

Opposite: **Pensioners line up outside the post office on pension collection day.**

RELIGION

BRITAIN IS OFFICIALLY A Christian country, although less than 20% of the population regularly attend church; many more attend sporadically on particular occasions such as Christmas Day, weddings, or funerals. Approximately 60% of the English people would classify themselves as members of the Church of England if asked to specify their religion. A non-denominational act of collective Christian worship takes place in all schools in England and Wales by law, although pupils of different faiths may absent themselves from this, and the nature of this act varies greatly across the country.

Above: **Many attend church services at Christmas.**

Opposite: **St. Paul's Cathedral was designed by Sir Christopher Wren (1632–1723). It is a Church of England cathedral.**

CHRISTIANITY

Many different types of Christianity are found in Britain, all with their own adherents.

THE CHURCH OF ENGLAND This church is the "established" or official church in England. The prime minister makes most senior appointments, in consultation with leading church figures; Parliament has a voice in its rituals, and the monarch is the nominal head of the Church. Except for the salaries of those in very public positions, such as the Archbishop of

Educate men without religion and you make them but clever devils.
—Arthur Wellesley, Duke of Wellington 1769–1852

Canterbury, and some state subsidies to the Church of England schools, no state funds are granted to the Church.

The Church of England is one of Britain's major landowners. Rents and income from this land are administered by the Church Commission and are used to pay clerical salaries and the costs of maintaining its many church buildings. Extensive renovations, increasingly necessary for many cathedrals and churches, are generally funded by local or nationwide charity appeals.

The Church of England is divided into two administrative provinces, Canterbury and York, each of which has an archbishop. Beneath them are a further 44 dioceses, each with a bishop. These in turn are divided into over 13,000 individual parishes.

The 574 members of the General Synod, a grouping of senior church figures, decides overall matters of policy by discussion and voting. For instance, the Synod voted to approve the ordination of women in 1992. Some disaffected Anglican clergy disagreeing strongly on this point have moved to the Catholic Church.

Church of England bishops speak out on matters of social policy—for instance, the Church of England publication *Faith in the City* is vocal in its criticism of government policies that have led to urban decay, youth deprivation and alienation, and widespread poverty and petty crime.

With decreasing church attendance, there is a dwindling supply of church personnel. It is common for a vicar to serve two or three nearby parish churches. Frequency of services and parish visits to the sick or disabled have diminished as a result.

Today the Church of England, or Anglican church, encompasses a broad range of Protestant practices, from the High Church, with its incense-burning quasi-Catholic rites, to the very Low Church, with its informal gospel singing and guitar playing.

HENRY VIII AND THE REFORMATION

The Church of England dates from the reign of Henry VIII (1509–1547). His first wife, Catherine of Aragon, bore him a daughter, Mary, but no son. As she became older, he applied to the Pope for permission to annul the marriage in order to marry a court favorite, Anne Boleyn, but permission was refused. Henry VIII split from the Roman Catholic Church and Parliament drafted new legislation making him supreme governor of the Church of England.

The split occurred just after Martin Luther's break with the Church, which led to the Protestant Reformation. Henry's initial split was purely on matters of authority rather than doctrine, so practice and worship followed the Catholic rituals closely. Later, during the reign of his son Edward VI and his second daughter Elizabeth I, the religious practice became more Protestant. Church services were held in English, with readings from the Bible, and communion in both kinds—bread and wine—was given to the laity.

THE CHURCH OF SCOTLAND As part of the 1707 Act of Union with England and Wales, Scotland was allowed to keep its own church (kirk). The Church of Scotland was founded in 1560 by the strict Calvinist, John Knox. The church developed into a staunchly Presbyterian organization and remains completely separate from the Church of England to this day. In 1990, there were 823,000 registered adult members of the church.

Scotland has well-respected Sunday practices, if not laws: no alcohol is consumed in pubs, no fishing or sports are allowed, and cooking, washing up, and even reading are considered sinful by the strictest adherents. A large proportion of the population attend church.

WALES There is no "established" church in Wales, but there is an autonomous Anglican church with six dioceses under a single province. It has approximately 120,000 members.

The bulk of Welsh Christians are Nonconformist or Methodist, followers of the 18th-century evangelist, John Wesley, whose message of hard work and thrift appealed to the growing working classes. The Presbyterian Church of Wales, founded in 1735, has 1,200 chapels, 180 ministries, and 75,000 members. As in Scotland, religious practice is severe and serious, and little work is done on Sundays.

OTHER PROTESTANT SECTS The Methodist community in Britain is not confined to Wales. A total of 450,000 adult members and a community of 1.3 million is spread across Britain, concentrated predominantly in the old industrial working class areas. It is one of what are known as the Free Churches, those which reject episcopal rule and hierarchical structures, concentrating instead on local leadership. The strictest Methodists are teetotalers, abstaining from all alcohol.

Other sects include the Baptists—167,000 people are registered as belonging to the Baptist Unions. The United Reformed Church, with 136,000 registered members, is a melding of the Congregational Church of England and Wales and the Presbyterian Church of England. The Religious Society of Friends, or Quakers, known for their pacifist views, has 18,000 registered adherents. Smaller sects include the Unitarians, Jehovah's Witnesses, Seventh Day Adventists, Christian Scientists, Spiritualists, and the Salvation Army, which

Evangelizing on the streets.

is best known for its social work—brass bands playing carols and anthems in order to raise money for projects such as soup kitchens for the poor and destitute.

ROMAN CATHOLICISM There are roughly five million nominal Roman Catholics in Britain, of whom 2.2 million are active. The Cardinal Archbishop of Westminster is the senior prelate, and the senior lay Catholic is the Duke of Norfolk. Britain has seven Catholic provinces: four in England, one in Wales, and two in Scotland, each with an archbishop; below them are 30 dioceses and 3,000 parishes. There are large Catholic communities in Liverpool and Glasgow, cities with large Irish immigrant communities; elsewhere local pockets of Catholicism sometimes date back to the days of persecution in the 16th century.

Historically, Catholics have been seen as politically suspect, owing allegiance to the Pope in Rome as opposed to the monarch of England. There were Catholic plots against Elizabeth I and James I, and Catholic supporters for Bonnie Prince Charlie and the Young Pretender in the 18th century. Even in the 1990s, it would not be possible for a monarch or heir to the throne to marry a Catholic without a major constitutional change.

Jehovah's Witnesses going from door to door, trying to convert people.

73

Above: **Muslims at prayer in Southall, London during the fasting month of Ramadan.**

Opposite: **Reciting from the Torah, the Jewish Holy Book, is an important part of the Jewish upbringing.**

OTHER RELIGIONS

ISLAM Britain's approximately 1.5 million Muslims make up its second largest religious group after Christianity. Pakistani immigrant communities found in urban areas in the Midlands, the northwest, and London have built their own mosques and religious organizations. Bradford, a Yorkshire textile town, has a very large Muslim community: it was here that protests against the novel *The Satanic Verses* by Salman Rushdie, reached their most explosive height in 1986; here, too, a Muslim "Parliament" has been established (with no constitutional rights or powers) to help Muslims gain a political voice.

British awareness of Islamic needs has progressed: test cases have been brought to the courts by Muslim girls who insist on wearing head scarves and remaining fully covered during school activities, and funds are now available and laws in place to allow the setting up of Islamic schools. While the Muslim community is predominantly Pakistani, there are Muslims from Bangladesh, India, Cyprus, and Saudi Arabia.

RASTAFARIANS

A large number of the Afro-Caribbean community are Rastafarians, recognizable by the green, yellow, and red colors often worn on "tams," or hats, and by their long dreadlocks hairstyle.

Ras Tafari was the son of Ras Makannen of Harar. He became Emperor Haile Selassie of Ethiopia in 1930, at a time when Ethiopia was the only truly independent black country in Africa. Deposed by a miltary coup led by General Teferi Benti in 1974, he died in jail on August 27, 1975.

Identifying Haile Selassie as the Conquering Lion of Judah and the King of Kings from the Bible's Book of Revelation 19:11 and 16, his followers started a movement in Jamaica in the 1930s and 1940s. This became popular in Britain during the 1970s, as some black communities rejected the Christian idea of accepting suffering in this life because of rewards in the next, focusing instead on the new religion that stressed black identity and its idea of African redemption. The Rastafarian view, that the drug marijuana is the "sacred weed" also referred to in the Bible, leads them to numerous confrontations with the police.

JUDAISM Britain's Jewish community has roughly 330,000 members, formed into 300 congregations in local synagogues. There are both Sephardim (from Spain, Portugal, and North Africa) and Ashkenazim (from Germany and central Europe); the latter are the most numerous. The majority are Orthodox Jews, and their chief spokesman is the Chief Rabbi; the minority are the Reform Jews. Jewish religious practice in Britain has declined over the last 20 years. Roughly one in three Jewish children attend Jewish denominational schools.

OTHER RELIGIONS Chinese communities in London and other big cities mainly practice Buddhism. There is also a Sikh community of roughly 500,000, and a Hindu community of 300,000. Bagwan monks, often dressed in red, orange, or purple, and followers of Hare Krishna, dressed in orange are popular from time to time.

A number of people, especially those in urban communities, have no religious beliefs and classify themselves as atheist, agnostic, or humanist.

LANGUAGE

THE ENGLISH LANGUAGE is the second most widely spoken mother tongue in the world with approximately 340 million speakers. English is the principal language in the United Kingdom, Republic of Ireland, the United States, Canada, Australia, New Zealand, the Bahamas, Jamaica, Grenada, Trinidad and Tobago, and Guyana. It is also the official language of several African countries, and is used widely as a language of commerce throughout the world.

Opposite and above: **There are dozens of magazines, national newspapers and tabloids in Britain such as** *The Times, Daily Telegraph,* **The** *Observer,* **The** *Sun,* **and** *Daily Mirror.*

The pronunciation, usage, vocabulary, and syntax used in different English-speaking countries vary greatly. Languages constantly change and develop, with new words for new concepts being added—for example, computer terminology has largely been invented over the last 20 years—and words falling into disuse or taking different meanings as circumstances change.

THE DEVELOPMENT OF THE ENGLISH LANGUAGE

When the Romans invaded Britain in A.D. 43, the native people spoke the Celtic language, then one of the most widely spoken languages in Europe. Under the Romans, Latin was spoken by the administrators and upper classes, but it did not filter down to the common people.

The English language was brought to Britain by invading Germanic tribes from the fifth century onward, who progressively settled the low-lying areas, pushing the Celts to the outlying mountainous areas of Wales and Cornwall. The word "English" comes from one of these tribes, the Angles, from what is now Denmark.

OLD ENGLISH

The language used in Britain between A.D. 450 and 1150 is referred to as Old English. Four different kingdoms existed from the fifth to the eighth centuries—Northumbria, Mercia, Kent, and West Saxony (Wessex)—each with their own language variations. By the 10th century, the West Saxon language became the official language, and most Old English manuscripts were transcribed in that area of the country. *Beowulf*, a 3,000-line epic poem, is the greatest surviving example of the literature and language of this period.

Like other Germanic languages, Old English nouns had cases and genders. The language was originally written in a series of straight lines called runes, which were easy to inscribe on stone or wood. Christian missionaries who arrived in Britain from A.D. 597 brought the Roman alphabet, which was widely adopted. As Christianity spread, with Latin used in church services, about 450 Latin words crept into the English language. These include "bishop," "abbot," "candle," and "angel." The Viking invaders of the 10th and 11th centuries added various Scandinavian or Old Norse words to the language.

The Norman invasion in 1066 had a huge impact on the English language, bringing thousands of French terms into everyday use. For nearly 150 years, the new nobility and most of the church hierarchy were French-speaking Normans until Britain lost control of Normandy (France) in 1204. These additions account for the rich vocabulary of the English language today.

MIDDLE ENGLISH

The language used between approximately A.D. 1150 and 1500 is today known as Middle English. During the late 14th century, English rather than

Shelta is the dialect used by the ethnic gypsies in Britain and Ireland. It is derived from Irish Gaelic and Old English, possibly via Celtic. Some English slang words are derived from Shelta. An example is the word "gammy," meaning "lame," which is derived from the Shelta word "gyami."

French was taught in schools and used in law courts. King Henry IV (1399–1413) was the first English king whose main language was English. By the early 15th century, the dialect of London had become a recognized standard as exemplified in the works of Geoffrey Chaucer, notably in the saucy *Canterbury Tales.*

An illustration of the knight(center), plowman (right), and the clerk (left) from *The Canterbury Tales,* which written in the 13th century.

PLACE NAMES

Many place names recall the groups that colonized Britain over the centuries.

• Celtic names are common for most English rivers: Avon is the Celtic word for river; Esk, Exe, Esk, Thames, and Wye are also Celtic words. London is a Celtic place name, after a person called Londinos. Barr means hill, torr means high rock or peak, pill means tide or creek, and the word "Llan" or "Lan" means church in Wales or Cornwall.

• Some Roman settlements are easily identified: towns ending in —caster or —chester, for example Doncaster and Chester, come from the Latin word, "castra," meaning army camp.

• Several Anglo-Saxon settlements can be identified by common suffixes in place names: "—ham," as in Chippenham, means farm, homestead, estate, village, or manor; "—leah," or "—ley" means woodland and subsequently, clearing in woodland. The suffix "—ing," as in Worthing, means people of. Finally, the suffix "—ingham," as in Nottingham, means settlement of Nott's people, and "—ington," as in Warrington, means farm or settlement associated with Warr's people.

• Scandinavian place names, found predominantly along the eastern side of Britain, can sometimes be identified by suffixes: "—by" means farm, as in Whitby; "—thorp" means outlying farm or secondary settlement, and "—thwaite," for example Applethwaite, means isolated piece of land.

• A few French or Norman place names can be identified and are often pronounced in a manner totally different from English usage: Richmond, Beaumont, and Beaulieu.

THE WELSH LANGUAGE

Twenty percent of the population of Wales speaks Welsh. Road signs and town names are all given in Welsh, often with very different renderings from the English names.

Welsh is a phonetic language, one of the Celtic languages similar to French Breton and to the Cornish language, which died out completely in the 18th century. The letters j, k, q, v, x, and z do not appear in Welsh; w and i can be both vowel and consonant—when used as a vowel, w is pronounced u as in "put," but when it is used as a consonant, w is pronounced as in the word "well." Y is used as a vowel, pronounced "uh." "Ch" is pronounced as in the Scottish "loch," "f" is pronounced "v," "ff" renders the English f sound, "dd" is pronounced as "th," and "ll" roughly as "thl."

The word "Welsh" means stranger. A few other terms are "dydd da" (thuhd-dar) meaning good day, "sut mae" (soot-may) meaning how are you, and "croeso" (kro-wee-so), which is used to extend a welcome.

GAELIC

Only about 75,000 people in Scotland speak Gaelic, and they are found predominantly in the Highlands. Like Welsh, Gaelic is also a Celtic language and was brought from Ireland to Scotland during the fifth century; unlike Welsh, the language has no official status in Scotland and is not taught in schools. Gaelic word order is typically verb–subject–object. For instance, "John buys cars" is expressed as "buys John cars." Gaelic words now used widely in English include bard, glen, bog, slogan, whisky, brogue, clan, and loch.

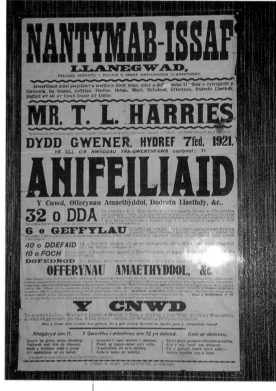

The Welsh newspaper *Nantymab-Isaaf* displayed at the museum in Cardiff.

ENGLISH DIALECTS AND ACCENTS

The way a person speaks is a good indication of where he or she comes from. A Welsh person speaks English with a musical, singsong lilt, while a Scottish person has a pronounced, almost guttural accent. Those who come from the West Country widen vowels and turn their "s" into "z," so that "cider" becomes "zoyder." Midlands accents from near Birmingham are flat and nasal.

Many of these local variations are the result of centuries of regional developments in the English language. For example, in a wide area north of the Humber river, across Yorkshire and over the border to Scotland, people still say "lang" rather than "long." In an area stretching farther south into Derbyshire and Nottinghamshire words such as "night," "right," and "fright" are pronounced with an "ee" sound as in "neat." The southern pronunciation of a long "ah" in "past," "path," and "laugh" never progressed beyond a diagonal line from the Wash in East Anglia to Wales; north of that line people tend to use a short "a" as in "flat" for these words.

COCKNEY RHYMING SLANG

A witty and sharp form of slang has evolved in the East End of London, of which many common expressions are now widely known in Britain and abroad. The slang depends on the rhyme on the last word of a pair; to add confusion, often only the first word of the pair is actually spoken. In this list, the words in square brackets are not said. Some examples will clarify this:

Rhyming Slang	Meaning
Trouble [and Strife]	wife
Butcher's [hook]	look
Whistle [and flute]	suit
Ball of chalk	walk
Dog [and bone]	telephone
Bowl of water	daughter
Apples [and pears]	stairs
Dicky [Dirt]	shirt
Half inch	pinch (steal)
Rosy Lea	tea
Cain and Abel	table
Jam jar	car
Sausage [and mash]	cash
Pen [and ink]	stink
Tit [for tat]	hat

Together with the age-old local dialects, Britain's immigrant population has brought further diversity and richness to English usage. For example, reggae and rap music generally feature in the rich English patois of the West Indian population.

Standard English, sometimes called King's or Queen's English, or Received Pronunciation, is the pronunciation generally practiced by those living near London and by most announcers on BBC television. Those from the middle and upper classes generally speak in this manner, with an accent that does not reflect where their family comes from. (Indeed, those of higher social class often come from more mobile background than those lower down the scale.) The richness and variety of pronunciation and accents is a major component of the renowned British sense of humor.

THE ARTS

BRITAIN'S VARIED ARTISTIC heritage is world-renowned, from the plays of William Shakespeare and the paintings of John Constable to the music of the Beatles.

Funding of the arts remains controversial. Public spending on subsidies to galleries, theaters, and universities has been reduced. Instead, businesses have been encouraged to sponsor theatrical and musical productions and artistic exhibitions, but in times of recession, less money is available for the arts.

CLASSICAL MUSIC

Early English music was mainly written for the Catholic Church. Thomas Tallis under Henry VIII composed music for the new Anglican church; his pupil William Byrd composed numerous madrigals, choral works, and string and keyboard works. In the 17th century, Henry Purcell wrote church music and harpsichord pieces, as well as the operas *Dido and Aeneas* and the *Trumpet Voluntary*, all of which combined the older medieval tones and scales of the English tradition with Italian and French styles to master harmony.

George Friedrich Handel, in London, under the

Opposite: **A modern sculpture titled Nana au Serpent by Nikki de St. Phalle in the Tate Gallery in London.**

Below: **The Royal Albert Hall in London is a popular place for both classical and modern musical performances, as well as sporting events such as boxing competi–tions.**

EISTEDDFODS (AYE-STED-FODS)

During the first full week of August the Royal National Eisteddfod of Wales [Eisteddfod Genedlaethol Frenhinol Cymru] is held. Its location alternates between North and South Wales, and varies each year. The word "eisteddfod" means a meeting of bards and the festival is a contest for poets, singers, and musicians. All proceedings are in Welsh, although instant translation facilities are available. The Gorsedd or council of Bards presides over the occasion, with the Archdruid of

Gorsedd officiating. At the end of the week two ceremonies are held: the Chairing Ceremony for strict meter verse, for which the winner is awarded the prestigious Bardic Chair, and the Crowning Ceremony for free verse, for which the winner gains the Bardic Crown.

Eisteddfods have taken place since the 12th century. Elizabeth I is recorded as having attended one during the 16th century.

patronage of King George I, composed the *Music for the Royal Fireworks, Water Music* and *The Messiah*. In the early 18th century, Thomas Arne composed *Rule Britannia*. During the 18th century, many philharmonic clubs, concert clubs, and choral societies were formed.

Late 19th-century composers include Arthur Sullivan, who teamed up with W.S. Gilbert to compose 14 operettas. Edward Elgar is famed for his *Enigma Varions*, his haunting *Cello Concerto*, and for the *Pomp and Circumstance Marches*, which echoed the self-assurance of colonial Britain. Ralph Vaughan Williams was inspired by the rediscovery of English folksongs and featured them in such works as *Fantasia on Greensleeves*. He also wrote six symphonies. Gustav Holst's orchestral suite, *The Planets*, a group of musical portraits of seven of the nine planets, was first performed in 1918.

Other modern British composers include Arthur Bliss, who wrote the *Color Symphony* in 1922; William Walton, who wrote *Belshazzar's Feast* in 1931; Michael Tippett, whose *A Child of Our Time* was written in 1941, and Benjamin Britten, who wrote the opera *Peter Grimes*.

POPULAR MUSIC

Two bands led British popular music onto the world stage in the 1960s. The Beatles had their first hit in 1963 with *Love Me Do*. The group dominated the British pop music scene until it split up in 1970, and their music had changed rock forever. The Rolling Stones released *Satisfaction* in 1965, one of many hit singles and albums spanning the next three decades.

The early 1970s saw the engrossing performances of bands such as T-Rex, Roxy Music, and Sweet, and colorful individual artists such as Elton John, Alvin Stardust, and David Bowie. By the mid-1970s, a division between teenagers and older rock fans was apparent. Adult-oriented rock groups of this time included Fleetwood Mac, Genesis, and Dire Straits. Meanwhile, the new wave or punk rock movement tried to reclaim rock music for the young and rebellious. Groups such as The Sex Pistols, The Clash, and The Stranglers outraged people with their rude behavior, spiky hairstyles, safety pins as earrings, and nose decorations. From the punk era emerged bands such as the Police, and Elvis Costello and the Attractions. Reacting against the punk movement were the new romantics bands such as Spandau Ballet and Ultravox.

In the 1980s came synthesizer rock and bands such as the Eurythmics. The British rock scene continues to be vibrant and exciting in the 1990s, with the sounds of rap and soul, changing the music scene yet again.

The Beatles—George Harrison, Ringo Starr, John Lennon, and Paul McCartney—from Liverpool. Their music, hairstyles, and taste in clothing were highly influential throughout the world at the height of their popularity.

LITERATURE

The breadth and richness of British poetry, prose, and drama, stretching over 10 centuries, can only be touched on here.

POETRY John Milton's 16th-century *Paradise Lost* conjures vivid images of Hell and Satan's fall from Heaven, while John Donne, who also lived in the 16th century, was a metaphysical poet, using wit and clever puns to convey complex ideas. The 18th-century Scottish poet Robert Burns used his local dialect to describe Scottish scenery and customs in poems including *Tam O'Shanter* and in songs such as *Auld Lang Syne*. Of the late 18th-century and early 19th-century poets, William Wordsworth's lyrical poetry about the Lake District and John Keats's romantic descriptive verse on the beauties of nature are well known. Early 20th-century war poets Rupert Brooke, Siegfried Sassoon, and Wilfred Owen all describe the horror of the trench warfare of World War I. The Welsh poet Dylan Thomas captivated the lilting musical quality of English spoken by Welsh people: the radio play *Under Milk Wood* is one of his more famous works. Britain has an official poet laureate, appointed by the Queen to write official poetry on state occasions. The current holder of this office is Ted Hughes.

PROSE Prose writers include Samuel Pepys (17th-century); Samuel Johnson (18th-century), who wrote essays on issues of contemporary interest; and Winston Churchill (20th-century), who wrote the *History of the English Speaking Peoples*. Novels became popular during the 19th century, with carefully crafted social observations by Jane Austen, romantic tales by Charlotte Brontë, gritty urban realism from Charles Dickens, and tragic rural pathos from Thomas Hardy. Twentieth-century novels include satires by Evelyn Waugh, tales of the sea from Joseph Conrad, working-class sensuality from D.H. Lawrence, and Graham Greene's movie-like narrative techniques. Prestigious literary prizes are awarded annually for original works of fiction, generating widespread interest in new writing. Novelists such as Salman Rushdie, Martin Amis, Julian Barnes, and A.S. Byatt are notable writers of today.

PLAYS British plays include the tragedies of Cyril Tourneur, the comedies of Ben Jonson in the 16th century, and the witty observations of Sheridan and Goldsmith in the 18th century. Modern playwrights include Tom Stoppard, who uses wit and pastiche, and Harold Pinter, whose writing includes themes of menace, hatred, and isolation. Alan Ayckbourn is known for his detailed portrayals of lower middle-class characters, and Alan Bennett, another keen observer of manners and mores, writes plays, television monologues, and radio pieces.

Portrait of the Polish-born English novelist Joseph Conrad, whose novels include *Lord Jim* and *Nostromo*.

WILLIAM SHAKESPEARE

William Shakespeare holds a central place in British theater. Between 1588 and 1613, he wrote a total of 37 plays, over 150 sonnets, and numerous poems. The Royal Shakespeare Company, founded in 1879, has two theaters devoted to his works: the Swan Theatre in Stratford-on-Avon, his town of birth, and the other at the Barbican in the City of London. While the language used is different from modern English, the themes and characters are vibrant and relevant four centuries later.

The historical plays, narratives of the lives of certain English kings, are thought to have been written in the late 16th century, during the reign of Queen Elizabeth I. They all help to explain her reign by glorifying her ancestors, such as Henry V and the Duke of Richmond (later Henry VII), and vilifying those monarchs they ousted, such as Richard III. Shakespeare also wrote several other historical dramas based on classical tales such as *Julius Caesar* and *Antony and Cleopatra*, using well-known plots but increasing their drama by adding tragic pathos to the central characters.

The comedies are generally light-hearted tales of love, with many a twist and turn before a happy ending. These plays often feature strong-minded women and somewhat ineffectual men, and rely less on plausible characterization or plot when compared to the histories and tragedies. They often contain observations on the lower ranks of society, often with humorous characters speaking in prose rather than verse.

Shakespeare's tragedies, in particular *Macbeth*, *Othello*, *Hamlet*, and *King Lear*, are his crowning achievement, all written in his later years. In each of them he develops a central tragic hero dominated by a fierce emotion that leads to his eventual downfall: ambition in *Macbeth*, jealousy in *Othello*, revenge in *Hamlet*, and pride in *King Lear*.

THEATER

London's West End is theater land, with over 100 theaters near Shaftesbury Avenue and Covent Garden. Mainstream musicals are popular, particularly those by Andrew Lloyd Webber. The Royal National Theatre on London's South Bank offers a wide range of contemporary and classical plays at its three repertory theaters. Many towns have theaters that either stage productions by their own companies or host touring groups. Fringe theater (not mainstream) is well represented on student campuses and in locations such as Stratford Theatre in East London, the Royal Court in Sloane Square, and the Lyric in Hammersmith. Manchester's Exchange Theatre also regularly stages fringe theater, as does Edinburgh's Traverse Theatre.

The Edinburgh Arts Festival every August presents all types of theatrical performances, both mainstream and fringe, to give opportunities to young playwrights to have their works performed. Chichester also has an annual summer theater festival. During the summer open-air performances of plays by Shakespeare are held in London's Regent's Park.

The West End is the heart of London's entertainment district. Shaftesbury Avenue is the center of theater land: the Lyric Theatre here was designed in 1888, the Globe and Apollo theaters opened in the early 20th century.

FILM AND TELEVISION

The "Ealing comedies" of the 1950s, including *Passport to Pimlico* and *The Titfield Thunderbolt*, were some of Britain's early cinematographic triumphs. In the 1980s, Richard Attenborough's *Gandhi*, David Putnam's *Chariots of Fire*, and Merchant Ivory's *Heat and Dust,* and *A Room with a View* were highly successful epics.

On a much smaller scale, the Scottish director Bill Forsyth's *Gregory's Girl* and *Local Hero*, Hanif Kureishi's *My Beautiful Laundrette,* and Chris Bernard's *Letter to Brezhnev* portray the less glamorous side of modern life and gained critical acclaim.

The British Broadcasting Corporation (BBC) has a reputation for well-produced television serials and soap operas. Such works include *Brideshead Revisited, The Jewel in the Crown*, Dennis Potter's *Singing Detective*, and soap operas such as *Eastenders*. The independent television channels also produce serials, soap operas, and films: Channel Four, in particular, funds films by new screenwriters and directors, and screens them a couple of years after their general release in movie theaters.

Britain has a strong tradition of television comedy, ranging from *Beyond the Fringe* and *Monty Python's Flying Circus* to *Spitting Image, Benny Hill*, and *Mr. Bean.*

PAINTING

Portraiture was the only branch of painting to survive in England after the Reformation, when religious works of art were prohibited. Under Henry VIII, Hans Holbein the Younger became court painter and depicted many members of the royal household. Nicholas Hilliard painted miniature portraits during Elizabeth I's reign, and Anthony Van Dyck painted memorable portraits of the early Stuart monarchs.

Britain has two museums dedicated to the history and development of cinema and photography. In London, the Museum of the Moving Image (MOMI) is at the South Bank Center, and the National Museum of Photography, Film, and Television is found in Bradford, Yorkshire.

During the 18th century William Hogarth painted sequences of moralistic scenes, decrying the sins of alcohol and other vices. Joshua Reynolds and Thomas Gainsborough both painted portraits of wealthy patrons, the former also depicting mythological and historical scenes, the latter trying landscapes. William Blake's mystical art had no following at the time, but its greatness was subsequently recognized in the late 19th century.

Britain's best-known exponents of landscape painting are John Constable and J.M.W. Turner. Constable's *Haywain*, painted in 1821, is an example of his search for truth and realism. In contrast, Turner painted nature as if it expressed human emotions, using light to highly dramatic effect in paintings such as *Peace: Burial at Sea*.

Many of these paintings are on display at the Clore Gallery in London's Tate Gallery. The Tate is London's most avant-garde gallery and frequently has highly controversial exhibitions. Every year the Royal Academy of Arts holds a summer exhibition of paintings by new artists as a showcase for upcoming talent.

A painting of the interior of the Crystal Palace, exhibited at the 1857 Summer Exhibition.

The Royal Pavilion in Brighton was built by the architect John Nash for King George IV when he was still Prince Regent. The writer Sydney Smith commented at the time, "... one would think St. Paul's Cathedral has come to Brighton and pupped [given birth]."

ARCHITECTURE

Britain's rich architectural heritage is highly varied, stretching back over 10 centuries of religious, civic, business, and domestic styles. The Tower of London and Durham Cathedral are examples of 11th-century Norman style. Exeter Cathedral shows the later Decorated style of English Gothic architecture (1350–1400), while Kings College Chapel in Cambridge, built in 1446, is done in the Perpendicular style.

Inigo Jones in the early 17th century developed the Continental Palladian style in buildings such as the Queen's House in Greenwich. Sir Christopher Wren, also a 17th-century architect, left a legacy of 52 city churches, including St Paul's Cathedral, which was built after the Fire of London in 1666, and another four churches outside the City of London. He was influenced by the Catholic Baroque architecture of the time, but evolved a more restrained form in his work. Sir John Vanbrugh's grandiose Blenheim Palace was similarly Baroque in style, as were Nicholas Hawksmoor's London churches, including Christ Church and the Spitalfields.

The curving Georgian-style Royal Crescent in Bath was designed by John Wood the Younger around 1775. The whole city is an architectural delight. Edinburgh's New Town is another example of the same architectural style. Robert Adam's Classical style is typified by Syon House in Middlesex. Striking examples of Victorian architecture remain in Sir Giles Gilbert Scott's St. Pancras Railway Station and his Albert Memorial; the Houses of Parliament, by Charles Barry, is also a fine example of Victorian design.

Sir Edwin Lutyens, designer of the colonial city of New Delhi in India, turned to creating dream-like country houses using arts and crafts techniques in the early 20th century. Modern British architects include Norman Foster, James Stirling, and Richard Rogers. Much of modern British architect's work lies outside Britain due to an innate conservatism among British town planners. Canary Wharf, a high-rise office development in London's formerly depressed docklands, was designed to create a new downtown area. However, an economic recession at the time it was finished has left the offices largely unoccupied.

The Royal Crescent in Bath is an example of classical Georgian architecture. Bath is one of the most elegant and architecturally distinguished of British cities. Many of its older buildings were bulit of limestone found in the nearby Mendip Hills.

LEISURE

SIR WINSTON CHURCHILL'S comment in 1938, that sport was "the first of all the British amusements," remains true in the 1990s. Sports are an integral part of the British way of life: millions of mainly male viewers watch soccer, rugby, cricket, and horse racing on television every weekend. Thousands more attend the weekly or bi-weekly soccer matches during the season (late August to May); others attend the summer international cricket Test Matches or the Wimbledon All England Tennis Championships.

Above: **Tourists and locals making the best of the summer sun on Brighton beach.**

Opposite: **Tobogganing in Richmond Park, London in winter.**

Participation in sports is also popular. At school, children are encouraged to take part in games of soccer, hockey, or rugby in the winter, and cricket, running, swimming, or tennis in the summer. Schools compete in numerous local leagues, as do towns, counties, clubs, pubs, and companies.

Sports funding remains controversial, with sponsorship a major part of most professional and even amateur sports. Proposals to ban tobacco advertising on television will have a devastating impact on many teams sponsored by tobacco firms. The costs of running minor league soccer teams are often disproportionately high, with increased safety standards, building requirements, and policing needs.

English soccer (its proper name is Association Football) is played throughout Britain, Europe, Africa, South America, and parts of Asia. The term soccer is a corruption of the second syllable of "Association."

SOCCER

According to the Sports Council, Britain had approximately 1.6 million soccer players during the 1980s. Played in schools, colleges, local boroughs, and in the national leagues, it is a very popular game.

English soccer is organized into two principal annual competitions: the League Championship and the Football Association (F.A.) Cup. The former is divided into four divisions: the Premier League and Divisions One, Two, and Three. Teams score three points for a won game and one point for a draw; the team with the most points at the end of the season wins the championship. At the end of each season, the bottom three teams in each division move down a division, the top two teams in each division move up. A play-off competition between the next top four teams decides the third team to move up a division. The last team in Division Three is relegated to a minor league.

The F.A. Cup is a knockout competition where teams must win matches to stay in the competition. There are separate Welsh and Scottish football leagues. England, Scotland, and Wales also take part in the European Championship once every four years. Individual teams take part in three European competitions if they qualify while the national teams take part in the World Cup held every four years. A cold afternoon spent watching a soccer match, with a cup of hot tea in gloved hands and teeth chattering against the cold is a truly British experience.

Soccer in England, as in other soccer-playing countries, is occasionally accompanied by incidents of "hooliganism," generally blown out of proportion by the media and the government. Some supporters do get out of control— often as a result of a bad decision made by the referee, or an unexpected defeat—but the majority of fans do not act in the same way.

OTHER WINTER SPORTS

The game of rugby was started at Rugby School in 1823. Rugby Union, an amateur game, has an annual series competition known as the Five Nations Championship that is played between England, Wales, Scotland, Ireland, and France. Matches for this series, and for international Test Matches against rugby-playing countries such as Australia, New Zealand, and South Africa are played on famous grounds: England's Twickenham, Scotland's Murrayfield, and Wales's National Stadium at Cardiff Arms Park.

Rugby League is a professional game and the players are paid. The game is mainly played in the north of England. Each team has 13 players instead of the 15 in Rugby Union, and the rules differ slightly for tackling and in other respects.

Hockey is played at many schools by both sexes; and lacrosse, another winter game, is mainly for girls. Cross-country running is quite popular.

A Rugby Union match in progress. According to legend, rugby originated in England in 1823, when a soccer player at the Rugby School in Rugby, Warwickshire, ran with the ball instead of kicking it.

SUMMER AND OTHER SPORTS

In the summer, tennis and cricket matches are played, and running, swimming, and water sports are popular. Tennis clubs abound, particularly in the southern counties. The All England Championships have been held at Wimbledon since 1877.

Cricket is a game played by two teams of 11 players on a large field, using a red leather ball and a flat wooden bat. The teams bat and bowl alternately. Runs are scored by two batsmen running between the two wickets—three vertical sticks in the ground known as stumps, and two smaller pieces of sticks (bails) resting between them. The batsmen can be out of the game in a number of ways such as by fielding positions that limit the number of runs made and by bowling strategies that bowl the wickets down. The team scoring the most runs wins the game. Test Matches (international games) can last for five days and still often end with a draw.

Horse racing and betting on races are fairly popular in Britain. Racing takes place from the end of March to the first week of November. Important races include the Derby and the 2,000 Guineas at Newmarket.

Formula One motor racing takes place at Silverstone north of London and at Donington Park in the Midlands.

British race-car driver Nigel Mansell in a Williams-Renault car at the Silverstone race track.

Races at the Royal Ascot are noted for the hats worn by spectators as much as for the racing itself. The Queen and other members of the Royal Family often have their own horses running in the Royal Ascot races.

National Hunt races, over hurdles or larger fences, take place between February and June. The most important races are the Cheltenham Gold Cup, and the Grand National at Aintree near Liverpool, which is the best-known steeplechase, local hunts raise money and run their own point-to-point steeplechases during this period.

Competitions testing the riders' skill at cross-country, horsemanship, and jumping take place at Burghley and Badminton annually. Horse shows are held across Britain during the summer months, ranging from small village contests to the Royal Windsor Show and the Royal International Horse Show at Wembley.

Greyhound race tracks are located in big cities. Large sums of money are bet on favored animals as they pursue a "hare" around a circular track.

Above: **Rock climbing is a popular pastime in rocky areas of the countryside.**

Opposite: **Accompanied by foxhounds, riders and huntsmen set out for a day's hunting.**

OUTDOOR PURSUITS

Walking is an extremely popular sport. Even in the pouring rain, groups of walkers clad in waterproof anoraks and Wellington boots, often accompanied by dogs, can be seen walking across fields, moors and along river banks. There are several long-distance footpaths, such as the Pennine Way that stretches for 250 miles from the Peak District to the Scottish border. Footpaths, bridlepaths for horseback riding, and tracks give walkers the right of way over much of the countryside.

Rock climbing is popular in hilly areas such as around Mount Snowdon in Wales, Froggatt Edge in the Peak District, Malham Cove in Yorkshire, and numerous locations in the Lake District.

For winter sports enthusiasts, skiing in Scotland is centered around Aviemore, although the snow is unreliable when compared to the Alps on the Continent. On a lesser scale, many families have toboggans to use on slopes in public parks and nearby fields in the winter. Many people skate on frozen ponds and rivers.

Sailing is popular, especially on the southern coast and on the Isle of Wight, where Cowes Week Regatta takes place in early August. Tall ship races leave from Plymouth, Falmouth, and Southampton in July and August. Dinghy sailing, windsurfing, and water skiing take place on some reservoirs and lakes during summer.

FIELD SPORTS

Hunting, shooting, and fishing are called field sports. Each sport has its season, arranged in order to allow the quarry time to breed. Fishing is by

far the most popular activity. Fishing spots range from canals and reservoirs to rivers where exclusive Scottish salmon can be caught.

There are several different types of hunting. Hunters meet and pursue foxes once or twice a week, between November and March, accompanied by huntsmen and followers on horseback. Between August and October, cub hunting, a less formal type of fox hunting, takes place. Hares are hunted using beagles or hounds. Deer are hunted with hounds in the West Country, where the sport is known as staghunting, and hunted in the Scottish highlands, where it is called deer stalking.

In all forms of hunting, the animals pursued—foxes, hares, or deer—are generally viewed as pests by the local farmers and landowners, who argue that hunting is the most natural method of reducing their numbers. Opposing them, hunt saboteurs, generally of urban backgrounds, find the sport revolting and barbaric, and do their best to confuse the scent and disrupt the hunts. They are usually not successful.

Oscar Wilde described fox hunting as "the unspeakable in full pursuit of the uneatable."

GARDENS

Gardening is a major hobby for many people. Many homes have a small plot of land, whether a suburban garden, an allotment at some distance from one's house or apartment, or a larger country garden. Newspapers have a regular column on gardening tips, and numerous gardening books line shelves of libraries and bookshops. A degree of competitiveness can take hold as neighbors try to outdo one another, and preparations for local horticultural shows can become webs of intrigue.

Over 3,000 individual gardens are open to the public under a National Gardens Scheme: these include ordinary suburban gardens and those of large country houses. Examples of Elizabethan knot gardens (left), medieval walled enclosures of fruit trees, roses and herbs, well tended mazes, 18th-century landscaped gardens, and cottage gardens with mixed vegetables and flowers abound throughout the country. Agricultural and horticultural shows are held throughout the summer months and classes in gardening and flower arranging are available in the evenings, which offer a wealth of ideas to the avid gardener.

VACATIONS

Most working people have four weeks or 20 days of paid vacation time a year, which they refer to as holidays. Workers in large manufacturing industries often must take their vacation when the plant is shut for maintenance, and many industrial towns have vacation or "wakes" weeks during the school vacations so that family members in different jobs can take vacations at the same time. Among workers in the service sector, vacation times are more flexible.

There are numerous vacation spots within Britain: the Lake District, Yorkshire Dales, and Peak District are popular areas for walking and climbing trips; Devon and Cornwall's rugged coasts and inland moorlands draw tourists from elsewhere in Britain as well as from abroad. The resorts

of the south coast are popular destinations for those from the Greater London area. Workers from the industrial towns of Lancashire used to go on vacation in Blackpool on the west coast, while those from the industrial towns of Yorkshire, on the other side of the Penines, used to go to Skegness on the east coast for vacation.

Many families take advantage of very competitively priced package tours to foreign destinations: Spain remains a favorite spot for British tourists, and many hotels on the Costa Brava offer British tourists fish and chips, strong Indian tea, and British beer. The Canary Islands, Greece, Italy, and other European destinations are also popular, and an increasing number travel to the Alps or to the United States for winter skiing vacations. In 1988, one fifth of the population took more than one vacation a year.

OTHER LEISURE ACTIVITIES

The British spend much of their leisure time engaged in home-based
activities: listening to music, watching television, playing video games,
and gardening. Making home improvements is a popular leisure activity
as well as a money-saving practice. The cliché that all British men wash
their cars on Sundays still has a ring of truth. Many people, generally men,
spend their weekends tinkering with motorbikes and cars, repairing or
working on their machinery in the garage and backyard.

Many British families have a pet, whether a dog or a cat, or a smaller
pet such as a goldfish or a parakeet. The British love of animals is
legendary.

During children's school vacations, visits to local attractions, theme
parks, and youth clubs are popular, although these vary by family and
area. Some schools, youth groups, and churches arrange holiday camps
and vacation activities for children. Organizations such as the Brownies or
Girl Guides also have vacation activities.

There are over 70,000 public houses or pubs in England and Wales, and several thousand more in Scotland. Pubs are major focal points of social life, formerly mainly for men, but increasingly for women, too. Pubs are open from Monday to Saturday from 12 noon to 11 p.m. On Sundays, they open from 12 noon to 2.30 or 3 p.m., and 7 to 10.30 p.m. Children accompanied by adults who wish to eat a meal are admitted to pubs at the individual landlord's discretion. Many pubs serve high quality food and a variety of snacks at reasonable prices.

Some pubs provide games for their customers' entertainment: perhaps a dart board, a pool or billiards table, sets of dominoes, and other board games may be found, along with pinball and slot machines.

Leisure time is a by-product of unemployment and recession, but for all the variety of leisure activities available, those out of work can benefit from only a few because of the expense involved. Libraries remain free, run by local councils, and have fairly wide selections of books, and in some libraries, records, compact discs, video tapes, and cassettes. Continuing education classes for adults are also available in a number of subjects.

A relaxed pub atmosphere is ideal for catching up with friends, socializing, and a friendly game of darts.

107

FESTIVALS

SEVERAL DATES ARE CELEBRATED throughout Britain. The beginning of a new year is celebrated everywhere, especially in Scotland, where January 1 is called Hogmanay. Traditional Scots eat haggis—spiced minced meat boiled in a sheep's bladder—before the "first footing," when a tall dark man from one household visits nearby homes bearing gifts of food, drink, fuel (usually a piece of coal), and good luck and wishes. He tries to be the first foot in the door in the new year. Another Scottish celebration, Burns Night, named after the poet Robert Burns, occurs on January 25: banquets are held with speeches, drinking, singing, recitations, and Scottish dancing.

Halloween, October 31, is increasingly being celebrated by small children dressed up in costumes and asking neighbors to choose between "trick" or "treat." November 5 is Guy Fawkes Day. Throughout England, bonfires are lit, old clothes are turned into effigies, and fireworks are set off to commemorate the failure of a plot in 1605 to blow up Parliament. The Sunday nearest to November 11 is Armistice Day, when a procession is held of 1,000 or so ex-servicemen led by the Queen and attended by political leaders. Participants lay wreaths on the Cenotaph war memorial in Whitehall, and two minutes' silence is observed in remembrance of those who died during the World Wars. Red paper poppies are sold for the benefit of war veterans at this time.

Above: **Fireworks over the city of Edinburgh on New Year's Eve.**

Opposite: **The Notting Hill Carnival in London. It was started by the the West Indians as a celebration of their culture.**

Above: **Two Chelsea Pensioners in full uniform and medals having a drink after the annual Chelsea Pensioners parade at the Royal Hospital Chelsea.**

Opposite: **Ceremonial guards waiting for the Lord Mayor of London to participate in the Lord Mayor's Parade in November.**

LONDON FESTIVALS

Several parades and occasions are peculiar to London and show some of Britain's pomp and ceremony.

Every February 16 there is a parade at the Royal Hospital Chelsea, a veteran's hospital founded in 1692 by King Charles II. Today's Chelsea Pensioners, often in their 80s, stand stiffly proud, showing numerous battle-won medals as they are greeted by a member of the royal family. In May, the Chelsea Flower Show takes place in the adjacent grounds of the Royal Physic Gardens, a show attended by thousands of amateur gardeners.

The Notting Hill Carnival, a street festival of floats, stalls, music, celebrating West Indian culture, has been held in north London on Easter Monday since 1966. It is a predominantly Afro-Caribbean affair, with steel bands, sideshows, and Caribbean food specialties such as goat curry. There is sometimes friction as local residents struggle to park their cars, and as petty theft increases with the crowds, and police must be careful to avoid provoking unrest. Recently, black community leaders have volunteered to nominate people from within the black community to police the event themselves.

The Royal Tournament at Earl's Court is an occasion for the various branches of the armed forces to compete in mock battle and daring races. The London to Brighton vintage car rally takes place every November, in celebration of the raising of the speed limit from 4 to 12 miles per hour in 1896. To enter the rally, cars must have been built before January 1, 1905.

One of the most spectacular London festivals is the Lord Mayor's Show, held on the second Saturday of November. The Lord Mayor of London, an elected official from the business community, riding in a gold state coach built in 1756 and drawn by three pairs of Shire horses, travels from the Guildhall to the Royal Courts of Justice in the Strand. The 12 great city livery companies, each with royal charters dating back several centuries, follow his coach in decorated floats.

The Lord Mayor's banquet is held in the Guildhall on the Monday after the Show. At other times of the year, he hosts dinners in the Mansion House. For all the centuries-old ceremony and archaic dress, the views of the City of London's powerful financial community are aired at these banquets, and political leaders use the event as a platform for their own policies.

CHRISTIAN FESTIVALS

During Advent, carol services are held in churches, nativity plays and pantomimes are performed in schools and theaters, street decorations appear in town centers, and many families buy Christmas trees to decorate.

Every family's Christmas routine is different, but most have a Father Christmas who fills the stockings children leave by chimneys or at the ends of their beds. Presents are exchanged with family and friends. A traditional meal of roast turkey, followed by Christmas pudding, is eaten either at lunch or suppertime.

Ash Wednesday, the first day of Lent, is so called because priests anoint their congregations with ashes to remind them that they return to ashes at death. Lent itself, the 40-day period before Easter Sunday, is a time when more devout Christians may make personal sacrifices to emulate Christ. On Maundy Thursday, the day before Good Friday, the Queen distributes specially minted coins—the same amount as her age—to poor men and women of her age at a different church every year. On Good Friday, churches hold services all day and devout Christians pray for the three hours when Jesus was believed to be on the cross.

The word "Easter" comes from the name of a Saxon goddess Eastre, whose festival was held in the spring. The giving of chocolate eggs at this time is more connected to the goddess Eastre than to any Christian belief. In some areas, egg-rolling contests are held on Easter Monday; in others, eggs are hidden in gardens and houses for children to find.

COUNTRY FESTIVALS

Several rural festivities date back over many centuries. In some areas, Plough Monday,

An elaborately decorated well in the Derbyshire village of Hope.

the Monday after Epiphany on January 6, is celebrated as the traditional resumption of plowing after the 12 days of Christmas celebrations have ended.

Appleby Horse Fair, a horse sale, is held every June in a picturesque village in the Lake District. A large proportion of villages and counties hold rural fêtes, shows, or contests during the summer months, generally for charity. Harvest festivals are held in churches throughout the country in late August, and churches are decorated with agricultural produce. In the West Country a Saxon custom of wassailing—wishing good health to the apple trees and cider drinkers—continues on January 17.

Morris dancing, a type of English folkdance, is a version of the European Morisca, a Moorish dance, came to be associated with May games (which takes place on May 1), and with the characters from Robin Hood (as seen in the dancers' costumes). The dance is performed by men, usually accompanied by music from an accordion and drums, and is said to have derived from pagan fertility rites.

The church took over many such pagan rituals. In Derbyshire villages, the custom of dressing the water wells takes place after Ascension Day in July and August. Pictorial panels of flowers are placed next to the wells to give thanks for the continued water supply. In Abbots Bromley in Staffordshire, a horn dance is held every September, an ancient fertility rite that dates back to Anglo-Saxon times. Twelve dancers portray various characters; six wear painted reindeer horns on carved wooden heads.

ROYAL PAGEANTRY

The British love of ceremony is best exemplified by the role of the royal family: their daily appointments are listed in the newspapercourt circular column, a column that lists the activities of the Royal Family. There are various regular and customary occasions when the public can view royal pageantry.

• The Changing of the Guard at Buckingham Palace takes place every Sunday at 11 a.m. The Life Guards and Household Cavalry are based in the Horse Guards Parade in Whitehall, where the soldier on duty is regularly photographed by tourists.

• The Trooping of Colours is held on a Saturday in early June to celebrate the queen's official birthday. The color, or standard flag, of each regiment has been symbolic of its fighting unity since the British Army was remodeled under Oliver Cromwell. The queen, mounted on a horse herself, inspects the troops of her personal guard.

• The State Opening of Parliament occurs every November, after the long summer recess; the ceremony has scarcely changed since the 16th century. The queen travels from Buckingham Palace in the Irish State Coach, and reads from the throne the Gracious Speech—a statement of the current government's legislative program for the coming year.

• Cannon salutes are fired from the Tower of London for the queen's official (June) and actual (April) birthdays, for birthdays of the Queen Mother and the Duke of Edinburgh, and for the Accession and Coronation days.

• Investitures of knights and other ranks take place throughout the year. Garter Day, an impressive ceremony at Windsor Castle held every June, is the day when any new members, chosen by the queen, are admitted into the Order of Garter (the highest order of knighthood).

• Irregular occasions are the focus of much ceremony: for example, the Queen's Jubilee Year in 1977, after 25 years' reign, was celebrated, although her 40th year on the throne was marred by the separations of two of her sons and the divorce and remarriage of her daughter, the Princess Royal. In happier times, royal marriages have been very grand ceremonial occasions.

FOOD

BRITISH FOOD has a reputation for being rather unimaginative and stodgy. While this description may be true of some school meals, many British cooks are becoming more adventurous. In Britain, as elsewhere, cooks are becoming more health-conscious when preparing food, decreasing the amount of fat used.

This openness to change is particularly true in towns, where produce is less fresh than in the countryside, and where pre-packaged cuts of meat and vegetables are readily available in supermarkets. The British still eat to live, rather than live to eat, but it is actually quite hard for tourists to savor the best of British food since much of this is cooked in private homes rather than in restaurants.

TRADITIONAL BRITISH FOOD

The traditional British breakfast is a very hearty affair, requiring a huge appetite and ample time. Grilled or fried pork sausages, sliced bacon, mushrooms, tomatoes, and baked beans are served together with fried, scrambled, or poached eggs, toast or fried bread. It may be accompanied by regional specialities such as lambs' kidneys; blood pudding, a type of rich sausage; oatcakes, which are flat, pancake-like items; or fried potatoes and cabbage, known as "bubble and squeak."

Not everyone eats a traditional breakfast. Those who do are usually engaged in heavy manual work, including laborers, farmers, and truck drivers. Most families have a more continental-type breakfast, consisting of cereal with milk and sugar (porridge in Scotland), followed by toast and marmalade (oatcakes in Scotland). Yogurt and fruit are also popular with weight watchers and the health-conscious.

Above: **A family having Sunday lunch. Sunday lunch is usually a family affair. It is a traditional and convenient time for family members to get together. People some-times invite friends to their homes on these occasions.**

Opposite: **A traditional butcher's shop offering a range of meats, game, and poultry. Many butchers wear hats for hygiene.**

117

Lancashire hot pot con-
sists of lamb, onions,
potatoes, and seaonings.

Some families eat their main meal at midday, others do so in the evening. The dishes served in either case are similar. A popular traditional Sunday lunch is a large joint of beef, mutton, or lamb roasted in the oven, accompanied by roast onions and potatoes, and other vegetables. Other British main dishes include steak and kidney pie; Lancashire hot pot, a type of stew; cottage pie, minced beef with a mashed potato covering; and toad-in-the-hole, skinned sausages baked in pancake batter.

Many traditional puddings are designed to fill up hungry mouths at minimal cost. Examples are bread-and-butter pudding, an egg custard poured over sliced buttered bread with currants and raisins; jam roly-poly, a rolled suet pudding spread with jam and usually served with custard; and rice pudding, long-grain rice baked in milk and sugar.

STEAK AND KIDNEY PIE

2 eggs
1½ lb lean stewing beef steak
4 oz. flour
1 teaspoon salt
½ teaspoon pepper
2 medium-sized onions
4 oz. mushrooms
6 oz. sheep or ox kidneys
½ pint beef stock (mixed with
red wine if preferred)

For the pastry:
8 oz. plain flour
1 teaspoon salt
2 oz. lard
2 oz. margarine
3 dessertspoons water

To make pastry: Sift flour and salt together, then rub the fat into the flour mixture until it looks like breadcrumbs. Add enough water to bind the ingredients together into a dough.

To make filling: Hard-boil the eggs, remove shells when cool, and cut into quarters. Trim excess fat off the meat, cut into half-inch chunks, and toss these in flour mixed with salt and pepper. Place in a 2-pint pie dish. Peel and chop the onions, clean and chop the mushrooms, and add both to the meat. Skin, core, and chop the kidneys. Add kidneys and eggs to the pie dish. Add stock to fill a quarter of the dish.

Roll out the pastry on a lightly-floured board and cover the pie dish, using an up-ended egg cup for support if necessary. Decorate the edges of the crust and brush with beaten egg or milk before baking in a hot oven, 220°C or 425°F, until pastry is brown, then lower to 120°C or 250°F and bake for about two hours. Cover pastry with wax paper or tin foil if necessary to prevent burning. Serve with boiled green vegetables and mashed or boiled potatoes.

Local specialties should be sampled when traveling in Britain: Scottish salmon is delicious, whether smoked or poached, and freshly-caught river trout is also excellent. Scottish beef, from cattle raised on the highland moors, has minimal fat and is very tender and tasty. Venison is also available in Scotland. Despite its description, Scottish haggis—sheep's innards, onions, suet, and seasonings boiled in the skin of a sheep's stomach and served with mashed rutabaga and potatoes—is a real delicacy. Tender Welsh lamb served with mint sauce and vegetables should not be missed. Oysters from East Anglia are a delicacy that is traditionally served only during months with an "r" in them.

A magnificent spread of food at Inn on the Park in London.

EATING OUT

It is fairly expensive to eat at a restaurant in Britain, and eating out has only recently become a part of social life. Families used to eat and entertain at home before going out for a drink and to socialize.

Numerous Italian, Greek, Continental, Chinese, and Indian restaurants can be found in most small towns, generally open late to catch people leaving pubs at around 11 p.m. who still want a drink or food. A few chains of steak houses serve traditional English food, as do some hotels. Some of the best quality and value in food can be found in pubs where, particularly in country areas, it is possible to enjoy very reasonable traditional English fare, and occasionally more adventurous Continental-style cuisine, served unpretentiously and quickly. Take-out restaurants are increasing in Britain. Chinese take-out restaurants are replacing many of Britain's traditional fish and chip shops, and kebab houses are common in many city suburbs. Hamburger chains such as McDonalds and Burger King are widespread and popular.

DRINKS

The custom of afternoon tea was established during the 1840s by the Duchess of Bedford. Gradually, afternoon tea was accompanied by small snacks such as homemade cakes, scones, biscuits, sandwiches, toasted muffins, or crumpets.

The British consume about one third of the world's total tea exports, averaging five cups of tea per person every day. The preferred brew is Indian or Sri Lankan rather than Chinese.

With 1,200 different brands available, beer is a national drink, made from hops, and matured in oak casks. Most British beer is bitter. Stout and mild beer are also available. A fairly high quality of bitter can now be found in most pubs, after the efforts of the Campaign for Real Ale reasserted the customer's need to drink traditionally brewed and kept ale. Real ale is always served at room temperature. Lagers, imported from Germany, Belgium, and Denmark, are increasingly popular, particularly among women. Like American beer, lagers are served cold.

In the West Country, cider is brewed from apples; some delicious rough local brews known as scrumpy are extremely strong. Wine is produced in Kent and Sussex in the south of England, where commercial vineyards have proved moderately successful in penetrating the local market. Strong homemade wines from elderberry or other wild flowers are best left to the enthusiasts.

Whiskies from Scotland's 100 distilleries remain a profitable export, and numerous blended whiskies and single and double malt whiskies are matured on Scottish islands such as Jura and Islay. Of other distilled spirits, gin from juniper berries is a profitable export.

Although afternoon tea is associated with England, it is not something most people have time to do. People drink tea at home or at work, but few have the elaborate afternoon tea.

121

Legend

- Capital city
- Major town
- ▲ Mountain peak

Height of land (feet)
- over 9000
- 6000 – 9000
- 3000 – 6000
- 1500 – 3000
- 600 – 1500
- 0 – 600

ORKNEY ISLANDS

SHETLAND ISLANDS

NORWAY

OUTER HEBRIDES

INNER HEBRIDES

North West Highlands

ATLANTIC OCEAN

Inverness
Loch Ness
Aberdeen

Ben Nevis (4,406ft.) ▲

Grampian Mountains

SCOTLAND

NORTH SEA

Forth

Firth of Forth

Glasgow
Edinburgh

Cheviot Hills

Tyne

N. IRELAND

Belfast

Isle of Man

The Lake District

Cumbrian Mountains

Tees

Yorkshire Moors

Pennines

Lancaster

York

IRISH SEA

Dublin

REP. OF IRELAND

Liverpool

Manchester

Mt. Snowdon (3,561ft.) ▲

ENGLAND

The Wash

WALES

Cambrian Mountains

Wye

Severn

Birmingham

Norfolk Broads

St. George's Channel

Cambridge

Oxford

Chiltern Hills

Felixstowe

NETH

Swansea

Cardiff

Thames

LONDON

North Downs

Dover

Bristol Channel

Mendip Hills

The Weald

Calais

BELGI

Winchester

South Downs

Portsmouth

Isle of Wight

Dartmoor

Plymouth

English Channel

FRANCE

ISLES OF SCILLY

CHANNEL ISLANDS
Alderney
Sark
Guernsey
Jersey

BRITAIN & N. IRELAND

Aberdeen   C2

Ben Nevis   B2
Birmingham   C4
Bristol Channel   B4

Cambrian mountains
   B4
Cambridge   C4
Cardiff   C4
Channel Islands, the
   C5
Cheviot Hills   C3
Chiltern Hills   C4
Cumbrian mountains
   C3

Dover   D4

Edinburgh   C2
English Channel, the
   B5, C5

Felixstowe   D4
Firth of Forth   C2
Forth river   B2, C2

Glasgow   B2
Grampian mountains
   B2, C2

Inner & Outer Herbrides
   B1, B2
Inverness   B2
Irish Sea   B3
Isle of Man   B3
Isle of Wight   C5
Isles of Scilly   B5

Lancaster   C3
Liverpool   C3
Loch Ness   B2
London   C4

Manchester   C3
Mendip Hills   C4
Mt. Snowdon   B4

Norfolk Broads   D4
North Downs   C4, D4
NorthWest Highlands
   B1, B2

Orkney Islands   C1
Oxford   C4

Penine Chain   C3
Plymouth   B5
Portsmouth   C5

Severn river   C4
Shetland Islands   C1
South Downs   C5
Swansea   B4

Tees river   C3
Thames river   C4
The Lake District   C3
The Weald   C4, D5

Winchester   C5
Wye river   C4

York   C3
Yorkshire Moors   C3

QUICK NOTES

AREA
England: 50,256 square miles
Scotland: 29,794 square miles
Wales: 7,967 square miles

POPULATION
55.5 million

CAPITAL CITIES
London (of England, Britain and the U.K.)
Edinburgh (of Scotland)
Cardiff (of Wales)

NATIONAL ANTHEMS
"God Save the Queen" (of United Kingdom)
"Hen Wlad Fry Nhadan," or Land of our
  Fathers (of Wales)

NATIONAL FLAG
Union Flag, popularly called the Union
Jack, as it is called when flown from a ship.

MAJOR RELIGION
Christianity (Church of England)

HIGHEST POINTS
Ben Nevis (Scotland): 4,406 feet
Mount Snowdon (Wales): 3,561 feet
Scafell Pike (England): 3,210 feet

CURRENCY
Pound: 100 pence to one pound sterling.
£1 = $1.50

LEADERS IN THE ARTS
John Constable (painter) 1776–1837
Joseph Mallord William Turner (painter)
  1775–1851
Sir Christopher Wren (architect) 1632–1723
William Shakespeare (playwright) 1564–
  1616
Jane Austen (novelist) 1775–1817
Thomas Hardy (novelist) 1840–1928
William Wordsworth (poet) 1770–1850

LEADERS IN POLITICS
Sir Winston Churchill (1874–1965); prime
  minister 1940–1945, 1951–1955
Margaret Thatcher (b. 1925); prime minister
  1979–1990

IMPORTANT DATES
1066 Battle of Hastings—last invasion of
  Britain
1588 Defeat of the Spanish Armada
1940 Battle of Britain

MAIN EXPORTS
Manufactured goods, machinery, vehicles,
scientific instruments, chemicals, and
pharmaceuticals.

GLOSSARY

ale	A bitter beer made from rapid fermentation of malt, hops, and yeast at a high temperature. Ale is generally served at room temperature.
barrow	Communal burial ground, generally found in chalk upland.
cricket	A game played by two teams of 11 players using a red leather ball and wodden bat. The teams bat and bowl alterbately.
constitutional monarchy	A political system that legally limits the actions of the king or queen In Britain, the sovereign's powers are mostly ceremonial.
Gaelic	Celtic language of Scotland and Ireland.
eisteddfod	Welsh poetry, singing, and musical competition during which all proceedings are held in Welsh.
devolution	The delegation of certain powers by a central authority to regional governments.
fringe theater	Theater companies that are not mainstream. They are usually small in size and many stage alternative and/or radical productions.
glen	A narrow secluded valley.
Home Counties	Counties that border London (Kent, Surrey, Essex, Hertfordshire, Buckinghamshire, Berkshire)
kirk	A church.
lager	A type of beer that is stored at a low temperature for several months for aging after it has been brewed. Lagers are always served cold.
loch	Scottish term for deep lakes (similar to Scandinavian fjords) that are found in the west of Scotland.
ria coast	A coast characterized by a series of long, narrow, wedge-shaped inlets that widen and deepen uniformly toward the sea.
rugby	A type of football played by two teams of 15 players each. The ball may be passed laterally or backwards, kicked forward, or carried to the goal.
tors	A high rocky hill or cliff.
weald	A forest or wooded area.
Witan	The Anglo-Saxon council that decided on royal succession and other policy matters such as relations with the Vikings and Picts and Scots.

BIBLIOGRAPHY

Great Britain, Insight Guides, Roger Williams (Ed), APA Publications (HK) Ltd, 1992.

Hiro, Dilip: *Black Britain, White Britain 1971-1991*, Grafton, London, 1992.

Kearney, Hugh: *The British Isles, a History of Four Nations*, Cambridge University Press, Cambridge, 1989.

McDowell, David: *Illustrated History of Britain*, Longman, London, U.K., 1989.

Paxman, Jeremy: *Friends in High Places: Who Runs Britain*, Michael Joseph, London, 1990.

The Cambridge Illustrated Dictionary of British Heritage, Market House Books, London, 1986.

Trudgill, Peter and Blackwell, Basil: *The Dialects of England*, Oxford, 1990.

INDEX

INDEX

INDEX

REFERENCE